Developing Home–School Partnerships

From Concepts to Practice

Developing Home–School Partnerships

From Concepts to Practice

SUSAN McALLISTER SWAP

Teachers College, Columbia University
New York and London

Published by Teachers College Press, 1234 Amsterdam Avenue
New York, New York

Library of Congress Cataloging-in-Publication Data

Swap, Susan McAllister.
    Developing home-school partnerships : from concepts to practice /
Susan McAllister Swap.
        p.   cm.
    Includes bibliographical references and index.
    ISBN 0-8077-3231-1. — ISBN 0-8077-3230-3(pbk.)
    1. Home and school—United States. 2. Education—United States—
Parent participation. 3. School management and organization—
United States.   I. Title.
    LC225.3.S9   1993
    370.19'31—dc20   92-40877

ISBN 0-8077-3231-1
ISBN 0-8077-3230-3 (pbk.)

Printed on acid-free paper
Manufactured in the United States of America

99 98 97   7 6 5 4 3

Contents

Foreword

Over the past decade, the field of school and family partnerships has grown in important ways. Research, policy, and practice have improved and advanced. This volume presents an excellent review of much that has been learned, and offers scores of practical ideas to help more educators take steps along the path toward partnership.

As the national Center on Families, Communities, Schools and Children's Learning started its work in 1990, we framed a new national goal: By the year 2000, "all schools should be ready for children and their families." This goal must be set and met by schools at all grade levels, not just schools for very young children. Schools must inform and involve all families, including those with different cultural backgrounds, to gain their ideas and assistance is helping all children succeed in school. This goal is attainable in the next eight years; it also may be a prerequisite for reaching other important national goals for students' higher achievement and attainment.

Susan Swap builds on this theme in *Developing Home–School Partnerships* to focus attention on important goals for all children's learning, including those educationally at risk. She discusses how schools and families share responsibility for increasing every student's motivation and success in school; and how, collectively, schools, families, and communities share responsibilities for the success with which this nation's students will be able to compete with students from other nations in the future.

The volume makes two notable contributions:

Swap explains important distinctions in approaches that avoid or promote full partnerships. She discusses what I see as three less-than-true, less-than-adequate partnership approaches: (1) a "protective model" that seeks to reduce conflict by discouraging contact—an anti-partnership approach; (2) a "school-to-home transmission model" that supports only one-way communication—a teacher-knows-best or benevolent-dictator connection; and (3) a "curriculum enrichment model" that limits involvement to parent support, information, and resources to improve the curriculum of the school and classroom—a necessary but not sufficient component of a comprehensive program.

She describes a better, more responsive approach—the "partnership model." It is the concept of partnership that enables schools to implement what I call a comprehensive program of six major types of school and family connections. The types comprise many practices that help families and schools understand and assist their children and each other.

Partnership activities help families obtain information on child and adolescent development, and establish conditions at home to support their children as learners at each grade level; conduct 2-way and 3-way communications (i.e., school-to-home-to-school and parent–teacher–student) about school programs and student progress; involve parents and others as volunteers and audiences; involve students and their families in learning activities and homework at home; involve families in school decision making; and establish collaborations with the community that assist students, schools, and families. While Swap groups these six types of involvement differently, their importance for program development is clear throughout the volume.

Swap describes a variety of practices to help educators begin to build their programs of partnership. The numerous examples Swap offers for each type of involvement are not strange practices, but are those that many educators presently are using successfully to build their partnerships with families. Swap offers particularly rich discussions of 2-way school-to-home-to-school communications, parent–teacher conferences, and how schools and families mutually support each other. Another topic that she gives significant attention is school-based management as a mechanism for guiding school restructuring and for organizing joint school and family decision making for school improvement.

The volume also helps us recognize that *there is more to do with this information and more to learn.* There are other investments that educators must make to implement good ideas about partnership, and there are many investments researchers must make to continue to improve knowledge and application of partnership activities and their results.

Without question, all educators and families should consider the arguments and practices that Swap presents, but their work would not be done. As our work with schools affirms, educators and families must assess their own school's starting place in practices of partnership, and outline clear 3–5-year goals for the six types of involvement. They also must organize leadership and a working team to plan, select, and implement practices tailored to the needs and goals of their schools and families, and evaluate their efforts. School and district personnel and financial support also are required. These steps, while formidable, can be accomplished with hard work and good will—two qualities of successful partnerships.

Swap notes in several places the need for new and better research for improving practices to involve families with diverse cultural backgrounds. She and her colleagues at the Center are working to build a deeper research base on this topic over the next few years. She notes, too, how much more we need to learn about the role of school and community collaborations that can strengthen families, student learning, and school programs.

Another topic that needs more attention are the links between research and practice in identifying the specific results that can be expected from particular practices or combinations of practices of involvement. All types of school and family partnership activities require communication, but for what reasons? to attain what goals? We are beginning to learn that, in the short term, each of the major types of involvement leads to different results or "outcomes" for students, parents, and teachers.

Not all practices to involve families lead quickly or directly to student learning, higher test scores, or more successful report card grades. Some activities, such as workshops for parents or information on child development or other topics, may lead *first* to parents' confidence about their supervision of and interaction with their childern. Other practices, such as new ways to organize, recruit, and train productive volunteers, may lead *first* to more effective supervision by adults of student activities, or to a more varied program for students of activities and perspectives. Still other practices, such as opening school decisions to input from parents or others in the community, may lead *first* to adults feeling attachment, support, and ownership for the school.

One type of involvement that may influence students' skills, scores, or grades in the short term includes practices that guide students and families in productive interactions about homework and other activities of student learning. Family interactions focused on schoolwork and homework may, if well designed, increase students' completion of their homework, so that they are more prepared for and perform better on tests that determine their marks and grades.

Some of the short-term outcomes of other types of partnership may, in time, increase student attention, motivation, and work in school. There are, however, several steps to cross between family involvement and improved student work and learning. For example, more responsive conference schedules may lead *first* to more parents attending parent-teacher or parent-student-teacher conferences. Over time, *if* the content of the conferences is pertinent, and *if* these conferences lead to good discussions and support between parents and students at home, and *if* this produces greater student motivation in school, *then* students may improve their scores or grades (as well as their goals, attitudes, and ambitions—also important outcomes). Over time, comprehensive programs should result in stronger school programs; a sense of community among educators, families, and students; more comfortable and confident parents; and students who are more motivated to learn and more successful in their work.

As educators and families work together to build comprehensive programs of involvement, they must consider whether and why they will choose particular practices for their own schools. Which practices will help them to reach the goals they set? There is still much to learn about the influence or results of specific practices and about the effects of combinations of practices. There is much to learn about the short-term and long-term results of partnership activities at different grade levels for students, families, and schools with diverse backgrounds, characteristics, and experiences.

These and other questions assure that school and family partnerships will remain a dynamic field. The partnership model is still evolving. It will be informed by the continuing, mutually reinforcing interests and investments of researchers and educators.

In *Developing Home–School Partnerships*, Swap offers a readable account, including personal experiences and observations, clear descriptions, and broad coverage of useful practices. This volume is an important reference for educators who are trying to understand how to proceed on the path to partnership.

Joyce L. Epstein
Co-Director,
Center on Families, Communities,
    Schools and Children's Learning
Johns Hopkins University

Preface

This book has been written to help parents and educators who are concerned about children's achievement in school. Partnership between home and school enhances children's achievement, and most parents and educators know that this is true. But fundamental questions arise as parents or educators contemplate reaching out: Can I bring up what's really bothering me? How much time will this take? Will he/she try to tell me what to do? What's the best way to approach the parent (teacher)? How have other people solved this problem? One goal of this book is to provide a conceptual framework and practical suggestions that will support the efforts of individual parents and educators to collaborate on behalf of children.

And yet, creating partnerships is not solely the responsibility of individual parents or guardians and teachers. A major theme of this book is that school/community cultures and district, state, and national policies create powerful contexts that influence individual action. In most settings in America today, these macro-forces do not support partnership. Understanding what these forces are and how they are maintained is the first step in changing them. The second step is to learn how others—not so different from ourselves—have created cultures that support collaboration. This book provides many examples of activities, programs, and policies in use in diverse settings that foster partnership as well as short- and long-term strategies for implementing them.

Another significant theme of this book is recognition and appreciation of the diversity in our schools and homes. The increasing diversity among families today accentuates the need for home–school communication to clarify possible differences of opinion about the values and practices that foster children's success in school. What we are discovering is that effective partnerships in diverse communities not only enhance children's achievement, but extend opportunities for the school to function as a site for learning and support for adults. Home–school partnerships in diverse communities are contributing to the creation of better schools that are both microcosms and forerunners of a new multicultural, multiracial democracy in America.

OVERVIEW OF THE BOOK

Explaining the urgency of the need for family involvement in schools and summarizing the range of benefits that involvement offers are the subjects of Chapter 1. In Chapter 2, I explore the resulting paradox of minimal outreach to parents by schools and the nature of the barriers that stand in the way of home–school partnerships. In Chapters 3 and 4, I present four models of home–school relationships that frame and organize interactions between educators and parents. Each model is defined by different goals, assumptions, and strategies.

The fourth model, the Partnership model, provides a new vision of home–school relationships in which parents and educators forge an alliance to create better schools and to support the success of all children in school. The first component of this model, establishing two-way communication, is discussed in Chapters 5 and 6; the other components, enhancing learning at home and school, providing mutual support, and making joint decisions, are the subjects of the next three chapters. The final chapter outlines three approaches to partnership that require increasing levels of commitment and proposes a sequence of activities for initiating a comprehensive collaboration.

ACKNOWLEDGMENTS

Many thanks are extended to the parents and educators whose candor about their experiences and willingness to risk change helped illuminate the process of achieving partnership. I am grateful to Barbara Jackson, Don Davies, Owen Heleen, Joyce Epstein, Vivian Johnson, and Jean Krasnow, colleagues from the Schools Reaching Out project, for their many insights in understanding the conditions that support change and their ingenuity and optimism in promoting it. Stone Wiske's perceptiveness in reviewing the manuscript helped to untangle intellectual knots and create the pattern that would weave together the final chapters of the book.

My colleagues at Wheelock who are working with me at the Center for Families, Communities, Schools, and Children's Learning provided perspective, vigorous argument, and information about the links between schools and families from different races and ethnicities. I am grateful to Nitza Hidalgo, Theresa Perry, and Sau-Fong Siu for sharing their wisdom and vision and illuminating the historical, economic, and political contexts of home–school relationships.

I am especially grateful to my children, Alison and Clifford, for tolerating my extended hours at the computer; and to my husband,

Walter, for his assistance in brainstorming, reviewing, and editing the manuscript in all its versions, and providing the space and encouragement to initiate and complete it. Susan Liddicoat's careful editing and graceful suggestions improved the consistency of the manuscript; the patience of my many friends at Teachers College Press made the idea for this book a reality.

Developing Home–School Partnerships

CHAPTER 1

Introduction: The Benefits of Parent Involvement

Home–school partnership is no longer a luxury. There is an urgent need for schools to find ways to support the success of all our children. One element that we know contributes to more successful children and more successful schools across all populations is parent involvement in children's education. When our focus is on improving the achievement of children at academic risk, partnership with families is not just useful—it is crucial.

Moreover, schools and children are not the only beneficiaries of partnerships. When families and educators work collaboratively, both experience new learning and an important new source of support. The strength and consistency of these benefits are strongly supported by the available evidence presented in this chapter.

THE URGENT NEED FOR IMPROVED PARTNERSHIPS

National statistics reveal increasing difficulties in educating our young people. Too many children are doing poorly in school, and most children are not doing as well as they could be. Levin (1987) estimates that currently about 30% of the children in this country are educationally disadvantaged and concludes that "these educational deficiencies later translate into poor life chances for employment, income, and political and social participation" (1988b, p. 2). An article in *Time*, highlighting America's "shameful bequests to the next generation," stated that a youngster drops out of school every 8 seconds (Gibbs, 1990, p. 42). In some urban schools, as many as half the children are dropouts, and even graduation does not guarantee more than minimal literacy in mathematics or the capacity to write a coherent letter.

Children of color, recent immigrants, and children living below the poverty line are more likely to experience low academic achievement and high dropout rates (Levin, 1988a). Higher birth rates, a new wave of immigration, and greater numbers of children in poverty are increasing the challenge to our schools (Edelman, 1992; National Center for Health Statistics, 1991; Levin, 1987; Swap, 1990b).

Even children who are college bound seem to be losing ground. SAT scores have been on a steady decline, and comparative international studies reveal that American children are not competing effectively with students from many other developed countries in their knowledge of geography, languages, mathematics, or science. The moral, educational, social, and financial burdens of this educational crisis are unacceptable.

An analysis of why and how we have arrived at this point is beyond the scope of this chapter. But practitioners and researchers who have created or studied models that have achieved educational success against the odds (e.g., Comer, 1988b; Schorr, 1988; Seeley, 1985) point to common ingredients in the solution. These include

- Partnership between school and community so that fragmentation of programs is reduced and the strengths of the community can be fully utilized on behalf of children
- Dedication to a common mission, which is most often success for all children
- Supportive policies and endorsement by the central administration, or at least the removal of bureaucratic barriers so that experimentation can be supported
- Recognition that strong relationships among children, educators, and parents are an essential requirement of comprehensive educational reform.

PARENT INVOLVEMENT AND STUDENT ACHIEVEMENT

Many different communities have experimented with parent involvement to improve student achievement. Some programs have been ambitious efforts at school reform; others have been on a smaller scale and aimed at particular goals, such as improving children's reading achievement scores in the primary grades. First I will provide a brief summary of the three major literature reviews on the topic. Then, for those who would like to gain the flavor of specific research studies, I will present summaries of representative investigations arranged by grade level.

Literature Reviews

The most extensive reviews of the links between parent involvement and children's school achievement were completed by Anne Henderson

(1981, 1987). She reviewed 36 studies in 1981 and 49 in 1987 (with some overlap). She concluded that "the evidence is now beyond dispute: parent involvement improves student achievement. When parents are involved, children do better in school, and they go to better schools" (1987, p. 1).

She explains that there is no one best way to involve parents, but "what works is for parents to be involved in a variety of roles over a period of time" (p. 2). The intensity of contact is important: "Public-relations campaigns, one-way communication devices, or dog-and-pony shows are not effective" (p. 6). She continues: "The form of parent involvement does not seem to be as important as that it is reasonably well-planned, comprehensive, and long-lasting" (p. 2).

In another major review of research on parent involvement and school achievement, Sattes (1985) cites positive effects on the achievement of children in grades K–12, either when parents are trained as tutors or when they are simply informed about and support their children's learning. She also reviews several studies that link parent involvement with increased student self-esteem, fewer behavior problems, and better school attendance. She concludes from her review of over 40 studies that

> Parent involvement impacts student achievement when that involvement is meaningful to parents. The highest achievement gains occur when parents are involved in preschool or elementary grades as home tutors. However, gains are also reported when parents are involved as supporters and reinforcers of their child's school learning and when parents are informed about their child's school progress. (p. 11)

Sattes further explains that programs are meaningful to parents when they can see direct benefits for their children; when they sense that teachers and administrators are committed to the importance of parents in the program; and when they feel that their involvement makes a difference. She also believes that parents "respond more positively if they can do something that is understandable, fun, and likely to be successful" (p. 21) and if they are not compelled to participate.

The studies cited in these reviews were conducted in a wide range of communities that spanned diverse geographic and economic conditions. Based on a review of the literature and her own extensive research, Epstein (1990) maintains that parents from all backgrounds and economic levels are willing to become involved in their children's schooling. She concludes that "the evidence suggests that school policies and teacher practices are more important than race, parent education, family size, marital status, and even grade level in determining whether parents continue to be part of their children's education" (p. 109).

Summary of Studies by Grade Level

Preschool. Several important research studies were conducted in the 1960s and 1970s to determine the effects of early intervention programs on children's IQ and achievement gains. This was the time when Head Start was initiated, and many other experimental programs, such as those developed by Gordon, Weikart, and Gray, were conducted during this period. In a review of many of these programs, Bronfenbrenner (1974) noted that the most impressive, long-lasting gains were made in a 2-year program where tutors worked with mothers twice a week to demonstrate toys and teaching approaches.

I will highlight data from two preschool programs with parent involvement components, which demonstrate gains in children's achievement not only during the program but also as the children matured. The Perry Preschool Program in Ypsilanti, Michigan, was based on a cognitively oriented curriculum and a home visit to each mother and child for one and one-half hours weekly (Berrueta-Clement, Schweinhart, Barnett, Epstein, & Weikart, 1984). The sample included 123 African-American children from low-income families, of whom 58 participated in the program for 2 years at ages 3 and 4. The program resulted in a significant increase in IQ favoring the experimental group that persisted through kindergarten and first grade, but disappeared at second grade.

A follow-up study, however, revealed that the preschool experience resulted in many important long-term benefits for the group: increased commitment to schooling through age 15; higher levels of academic motivation; decreased placement in special education classes; increased scholastic achievement as measured by grades and performance on achievement tests; less unemployment; higher levels of employment; higher earnings by age 19; and fewer contacts with the criminal justice system, including fewer arrests. Berrueta-Clement et al. (1984) speculated that the involvement of parents in their children's early education provided the sustaining link that maintained the benefits of the preschool training, but they did not have sufficient evidence in this study to support that hypothesis.

From 1968 to 1971, 600 children participated in a preschool program called Project HOPE in rural Appalachia (Gotts, 1980). The children were from small, lower-middle-class communities. There were three program elements: daily television lessons and weekly printed parent guides (TV); weekly home visits from a local trained paraprofessional who demonstrated how to teach the child, helped problem-solve, and connected parents with resources (HV); and a group experience for the child and other children one half-day a week (GE). Children were in three different treatment conditions: TV only, TV plus HV, and TV plus HV plus GE. All three treatment groups outperformed the controls on the Appalachia Preschool Test (APT), a test of conceptual development. The HV groups also outperformed the control and TV only group on the APT, the Peabody Picture Vocabulary Test, and parts of the Frostig and Illinois Test of Psycholinguistic Ability.

A follow-up study begun in 1975, when the children had reached grades 3–7, revealed that the children who received home visiting were doing better than the TV only group in school attendance, grade point average, and total basic skills scores on a standardized test given to children in third grade. A second follow-up study begun in 1977, when the children were in grades 5–9, indicated that home-oriented instruction resulted in fewer emotional and behavior problems, fewer retentions in grade, and higher scores for parents on an index called "generativity," which measured the "parenting role of caring for and nurturing their children toward psychosocial maturity" (Gotts, 1980, p. 233). Gotts concluded that "the present findings confirm . . . what many parent educators already believe about the importance of involving parents in their children's early education" (p. 234).

Elementary Level. A Parent Education Follow-Through Program (PEFTP) was designed by Gordon and associates to serve low-income children and their families in grades K–3 (Olmstead & Rubin, 1983). This program was begun in 1969 and was still operating in eight communities in 1983. The parent involvement program had three components. Home visits were made by program parents employed as paid professional aides who spent half of their time working as classroom instructional personnel and the other half visiting the homes of children in their classroom. During the visits, information was exchanged about home and school, and a home learning activity was shared that stressed specific teaching behaviors (e.g., asking questions that have more than one right answer; getting the learner to ask questions). A second component of the program was encouraging parents to participate in the school in any of six roles: as teacher of their own child, paid paraprofessional, decision-maker through the Policy Advisory Committees, adult learner, audience, and classroom volunteer. A third component of the PEFTP was ensuring that participants had access to a comprehensive array of social, psychological, and health services.

Olmstead and Rubin (1983) reported on four evaluation studies that specifically linked parent behaviors to child achievement. Although the details of the four studies are too complex to review completely here, they were all unusual in studying the effects of the programs on parents as well as children through either direct observations of parents' interactions with children or interviews. All four studies showed significant relationships between parental measures and child achievement. For example, in one study, program parents were observed teaching their children, and their rate of use of the Desirable Teaching Behaviors (DTBs) was compared with controls. The investigator found that program parents used significantly more DTBs than control parents and that there was a significant correlation between the number of DTBs used by parents and children's scores on the total reading and math subtests of the Stanford Achievement Test.

In their conclusion, the authors emphasized the strong relationship between parent involvement and child school performance, the willingness of parents to be active participants in their children's education, and the importance of increasing the active participation of parents in schools.

Another study (Trovato & Bucher, 1980) reported on the utility of involving parents simply as reinforcers of their children's learning during a 15-week pilot program to improve children's reading scores. Children were assigned to a control group, a peer tutoring group, or a peer tutoring group plus home reinforcement. The authors found that when the school contacted parents by telephone or letter (average total contact was one hour per family) to inform them about their children's progress, the children performed better on the Stanford Reading Achievement Test than did either the control group or the group that had experienced peer tutoring but no parental reinforcement. For example, reading comprehension scores (expressed in average yearly gain) were twice as high for the peer tutoring plus parental reinforcement group than for the peer tutoring alone group (1.04 vs. .50).

A study was conducted in an elementary school in Chicago to evaluate the effects of an intensified parent involvement program on children's reading achievement scores (Walberg, Bole, & Waxman, 1980). The children were African-American and from poor families (80% in public housing and receiving aid for dependent children; 75% single-parent families). A joint parent–staff steering committee formulated seven goals for the project, and seven 10-member staff–parent committees were appointed that met periodically during the summer and school year to plan and guide the accomplishment of the goals.

The committees and staff drafted a staff–parent–child contract to be followed during the school year. Parents pledged such things as working for the highest goals within the child's reach, providing a quiet, well-lighted place for regular study, encouraging the child by talking with him or her daily, offering compliments on progress, and cooperating with the teacher on school work, discipline, and attendance. It is important to note that fewer than 1% of the children had unsigned contracts (which were also signed by the district superintendent, principal, and classroom teacher).

Parents were provided with a booklet describing school policies and activities that encouraged reading. Several book fairs were held at the school to enable parents to buy and trade books for their children. Average scores on the Iowa Test of Basic Skills went up throughout the school, but in classes where teachers were especially committed to parent involvement, average gains were .5 to .6 grade equivalents higher than for students whose teachers and parents were less intensively involved (average gain for intensively involved parents was 1.1 grade equivalents). The authors concluded that parent programs initiated in the schools may be as effective, less costly, and as capable of sustaining gains throughout the elementary years as child-centered or home-based enrichment programs.

A provocative study in England (Tizard, Schofield, & Hewison, 1982) compared the effects of two special programs on children's reading achievement scores. They found that elementary-age children who read aloud to their parents 2–4 times a week using books sent home from school showed highly significant gains in reading achievement compared with students with no intervention or even with students who were provided with a special teacher who listened to them read and offered tutorial assistance in school.

Parent involvement programs are not always successful in improving children's school achievement. A study by Mehran and White (1988) invited parents of kindergarten children in Title I schools to participate in an experimental parent tutoring program. The children had been identified as at risk for learning to read. Of the 80 parents invited, 76 agreed to join, and these were randomly assigned to either an experimental or a control group.

The program was very ambitious: Parents were asked to come to two 4-hour training sessions in July, follow-up meetings twice a week during the rest of the summer, and additional meetings once a month during the school year. Parents were asked to tutor their children in sounds and letters, basic sight words, blending of sounds, and other prereading skills for 15 minutes three times a week from August to April. They were also asked to submit tutoring logs every 2 weeks and seek additional assistance if they were having difficulty with the tutoring techniques.

The program had no overall effects on the reading achievement scores of the children. However, only eight of the original 38 parents were able to complete the program. These eight did make significant gains in reading achievement. The study raises interesting questions about the types of parent involvement programs that are likely to be successful, especially when 76 out of 80 parents were originally eager to support their children's learning at home. Possible factors in most parents' unwillingness or inability to complete this program may have been that it placed parents in a very traditional "teacher" role (as opposed to a role in which they might enrich or support the classroom curriculum), the complexity of the training, and/or the time requirements for tutoring and record keeping.

Secondary Schools. Although studies of family involvement in secondary schools are not prominent in the literature, a study by Duncan (1969) reported by Sattes (1985) yielded very positive results. Sattes reports:

> Counselors met individually with all parents the summer before their children entered junior high school. After three years these students were compared to the class who had entered the year before, for whom no individual parent meetings had been held except by request. Average daily attendance was different at the .001 level of significance, favoring the group whose parents were met individually. In addition, students' mean grade point average was higher; there were fewer school dropouts (two versus eight); and the parents continued to be more involved. During their children's three years of junior high, the parents made significantly more contacts with school staff. Only 13% made no contact at all, compared to 73% of a comparison group. (p. 13)

Moses, Kamii, Swap, and Howard (1989) reported on a Cambridge, Massachusetts, program that relied on parent support to improve the achievement of seventh and eighth graders in mathematics so that all students would have access to the college preparatory mathematics curriculum of the high school. A cornerstone of the "Algebra Project" became

> the expectation that every child in the Open Program could achieve math literacy, an ethos powerful enough to suffuse both peer and adult culture. The components of this effort included changing the content and methods of teaching math, involving parents in activities that would better enable them to support their children's learning, teaching students to set goals and motivating them to achieve, and reaching out to Black college graduates in the Boston area who would serve as tutors and role models of academic success. (p. 428)

The project produced its first full graduating class in the spring of 1986. Not a single student was placed in lower level math courses in the high school, and 39% of the graduates were placed in honors courses. For the first time, African-American and female students from this school were included in the honors high school mathematics courses.

Parent involvement was considered essential to the success of the program and was sought in several ways: The leader of the project was himself a parent in the community; informational meetings were held regularly for parents; parents had an opportunity to indicate whether they thought their child should be included in the nontracked "Algebra Project" program (all parents requested this opportunity); parents participated in workshops on increasing student motivation, achievement, and self-esteem; parents were invited to join "Honors Bound" parent groups, which prepared students of color to accept the challenge of taking honors courses in high school and created a home–school culture that would nurture and support serious intellectual effort; parents were involved as volunteers in the classroom and were themselves invited to take a Saturday morning class in algebra.

It is hard to know, of course, which interventions were most critical in creating the extraordinary burst in mathematics achievement that occurred (and has continued with succeeding groups of students in this school), but both parents and educators felt that the "community organizing" effort was an essential component of the students' success.

Overcoming Ceiling Effects

Henderson (1987) points out that although meaningful parent involvement is consistently effective in raising children's achievement scores, in poor districts parental support may encounter a ceiling effect. That is, parental involvement raises their children's achievement scores, but not to the national average. In addition, research in elementary and secondary schools often focuses on time-limited programs, where gains are recorded for the period of the innovation, but long-term structural modifications to maintain those gains for subsequent students are not made.

These barriers have been overcome most convincingly when parent involvement programs are integrated with a comprehensive plan for school improvement. The most widely known example of this strategy is the Comer model (Comer, 1988a), which has been initiated in over 120 inner city schools across the country (recently including middle and high schools). In many of the poor inner city schools that use the "School Development Program" or "Comer process," achievement scores have reached or surpassed the national average, and students have maintained those gains over several years.

The Comer process requires structural changes in the school that support school improvement. The School Planning and Management Team is a structural innovation in which parents, administrators, and staff are responsible for initiating and monitoring school-wide policies and programs. The Staff and Student Support Team is another required structure that offers comprehensive, interdisciplinary support and problem solving to meet the needs of children and staff. Parents participate on the School Planning and Management Team, and parent support and involvement, considered essential to the model, are vigorously sought through a variety of additional roles and activities at school and at home. Because the Comer process *is* a transforming process that affects attitudes, philosophy, structures, and day-to-day practices, it is not an innovation that has a short life in schools.

EFFECTS OF PARENT INVOLVEMENT ON ADULTS

Parents and educators reap benefits from collaboration. In programs where parents and teachers work successfully together, teachers report experiencing support and appreciation from parents and a rekindling of their own enthusiasm for problem solving (Swap, 1987). Research evidence also confirms that teachers report more positive feelings about teaching and about their school when there is more parent involvement at the school (Epstein & Dauber, 1991; Leitch & Tangri, 1988). Teachers are impressed by the mutuality of interests and find that collaboration both broadens their perspective and increases their sensitivity to varied parent circumstances. (As an illustration, Epstein, 1985, found that teachers who were leaders in parent involvement made equal demands on single and married parents and rated them as equally helpful and responsible in conducting learning activities at home, while teachers who were not leaders required more from single parents and rated them as less helpful and responsible.)

Parents report pleasure in getting to know teachers as people, express a new appreciation for the commitment and skill of teachers, and may (depending on the program content) experience an increase in their own parenting skills and confidence in them (Swap, 1987, 1990c). In a survey of over 1,200 parents, Epstein (1990) discovered that parents whose children's teachers were leaders in parent involvement were significantly more likely than other parents to feel they received many ideas of how to help their children at home, to believe that they understood more about their children's curriculum, and to feel more positively about the teacher's interpersonal skills and teaching ability.

For both parents and teachers, collaboration reduces the characteristic isolation of their roles. For parents, knowing that teachers share their concerns about their children is very reassuring; for teachers, knowing that a parent recognizes the complexity of their role in the classroom is comforting. When parents and teachers work on school improvement tasks together, there is pleasure in discovering the power of their own voices to create change beyond the classroom and pride in contributing to goals that are shared by the community (Krasnow, 1990b).

Collaboration increases the resources available to schools and parents. For example, parents may contribute to schools as volunteers or paid aides, helping to individualize and enrich student work. Parents' expertise may help a school design and build a playground or computer laboratory. Parents' knowledge of a community's history or their own culture may enhance or clarify classroom curriculum. Parents may provide linkages to partnerships with businesses, agencies, cultural institutions, or other resources in the community. Parents can be a political asset when they advocate on behalf of children and schools at school board meetings or in legislative sessions. In addition, schools may provide parents with educational programs, new skills, access to community services, and valuable informal connections with others in the community.

SUMMARY

National assessments reveal an increasingly urgent need for the improvement of educational outcomes for our nation's children. The data reviewed on the connections between parent involvement and student achievement point unambiguously to the strength of this relationship across a range of settings and conditions. The studies suggest that parents are very willing to become involved in school or home-based learning activities when the activities are meaningful, congruent with family priorities, and likely to be useful. Although Henderson (1987) points to a ceiling effect on the power of parent involvement to increase student achievement in low-income, urban schools, some comprehensive programs of which parent involvement is a part (e.g., "Comer" schools and others to be described in Chapter 4) may transcend this constraint.

Though not a focus of this chapter, reviews of the literature also indicate that parent involvement often promotes other student outcomes such as improved self-esteem, attendance, and behavior. Parent involvement programs also benefit adults. Collaboration generally results in increased individual support for teachers and parents, as well as feelings of satisfaction at contributing to important changes in children or programs. Parent involvement also increases the resources available to children, adults, and the school, and often leads to collaborations with businesses or agencies within the community.

Given the widespread recognition that parent involvement in schools is important, that it is unequivocally related to improvements in children's achievement, and that improvement in children's achievement is urgently needed, it is paradoxical that most schools do not have comprehensive parent involvement programs. In Chapter 2, we will examine the barriers to home-school partnership that have kept collaboration to a minimum.

CHAPTER 2

Barriers to Parent Involvement

In theory, parents and teachers agree on the importance of parent involvement and home–school partnership. A poll taken by the National Education Association found that 90% of teachers across the country and at all grade levels thought that more home–school interaction would be beneficial (Moles, 1982). Joyce Epstein discovered that almost all parents, even those from the most economically depressed communities, are committed to their children's education. She concluded: "Parents say they want their children to succeed; they want to help them; and they need the school's and teacher's help to know what to do with their children at each grade level" (Brandt interviewing Epstein, 1989, p. 27).

One would think that with both teachers and parents supporting the principle of home–school partnership and with data confirming its benefits such programs would be universal—or at least commonplace. The paradox is that parent involvement in the schools is surprisingly minimal. In a review of the literature on parent participation, Epstein (1990) concluded that "most parents cannot and do not participate at the school building, [and] . . . few parents participate directly in school decision-making as leaders or representatives of other parents" (p. 108). The National Center for Education Statistics surveyed 24,600 eighth graders in 1,000 public and private schools across the country. Their data, presented in the "National Educational Longitudinal Survey of 1988," revealed that half of the parents had not attended a school meeting during the year, and barely one third belonged to parent-teacher organizations (Hafner, 1990).

How can we account for this paradoxical state of affairs? Despite the urgent need for partnership and the weight of supportive evidence, parents continue to be kept at a distance in most schools. One must conclude that there are powerful barriers that are inhibiting educators from reaching out to parents. In this chapter, four of these barriers will be explored as the first step in overcoming them. These barriers are changing demographics, school norms that do not support partnerships, limited resources to support parent involvement, and lack of information about how to establish partnerships.

CHANGING DEMOGRAPHICS

The Data

Families have been changing very rapidly in the last few decades. Most are aware of the changes, but the extent and rapidity of the transformation are quite astonishing. For example, 70% of mothers of school-aged children are now in the work force compared with 30% in 1960. Almost half of all marriages end in divorce. There are more single-parent families: 25%, double the figure in 1970. A third of all marriages are now remarriages, and one out of four children has one or more step-parents (Braun & Swap, 1987). The number of children having children has increased dramatically in the last decade, particularly among children under 15 (National Center for Health Statistics, 1991).

The number of children living in poverty is increasing. Almost one in four children now lives below the poverty line, and over half of the children living in single-parent families are poor (for a fuller discussion of these statistics, see Braun & Swap, 1987). According to a Children's Defense Fund study (1989), the rate of poverty among families with young children almost doubled between 1973 and 1986.

It is important to note that changing demographics have not bypassed educators. Most teachers have families of their own, and the stresses of divorce, step-parenting, and declining spending power are built into the fabric of many teachers' lives.

Racial, language, and ethnic diversity are more common in our classrooms. By the year 2000, the Census Bureau projects that the total number of minority children will have increased by 25.5% from 1985 levels and that the proportion of all children who are members of minority groups will have increased from 28% to 33% (Children's Defense Fund, 1989, p. 116). Immigration figures are soaring. We are experiencing the highest immigration levels since the 1920s. According to preliminary data from the 1990 census, immigrants now account for 30% of the nation's population growth, up from 19% in 1980 (Sege, 1990, pp. 1, 18). Moreover, there is a shift from traditional lands of origin, with more children now coming from Mexico, Asia, Central and South America, and the Caribbean (First & Carrera, 1988).

Effects of the Demographic Changes

All these changes have made educating children more complicated. The stress of families experiencing separation and divorce affects the behavior and performance of children in classrooms. Poverty, early parenthood, and parental addiction can influence the readiness of children for learning. The relative unavailability of mothers employed outside the home limits their helpfulness during school hours and results in less supervision of children after school. Many educators feel angry at these changing conditions and blame parents for devoting less energy to their children's education and well-being. Samuel Sava, executive director of the National Association of Elementary School Principals, expresses this view clearly.

> This family revolution is the greatest single cause of the decline in student achievement during the last 20 years. It's not better teachers, texts, or curricula that our children need most; it's better childhoods, and we will never see lasting school reform until we first see parent reform (Bacon, 1990, p. B1).

Educators who have this orientation (and many do) generally feel that since it is the parents who are failing to meet their responsibilities to today's children, it is not the school's responsibility to reach out to parents in new ways. Perhaps of even more concern is the common observation that when parents do not respond to traditional forms of outreach (e.g., morning parent association meetings, open houses, brief conferences at school), the assumption is that "parents today don't care" about their children or their schooling. As I will explain later, I think both assumptions are destructive and inaccurate.

Because demographic changes also affect educators, their availability for meetings before or after school also cannot be taken for granted, especially when their time is not compensated or when special arrangements for child care need to be made. Teaching, like parenting, is not an easy job. Yet expectations for teachers' performance have been increasing despite more complex teaching environments and declining community support for schools. For all these reasons, taking on the additional responsibility of reaching out to parents in new ways may not feel rewarding to educators.

The increase in the diversity of our students has also created many challenges for educators, as my own visits to several schools have underscored. In Chelsea, Massachusetts, for example, 70% of the children now come from homes where English is not the primary language spoken. In a public school in La Jolla, California, 31 different primary languages are spoken by the children (Swap, 1990c). In many cases, the diversity in the student body is enriching to the class, the teacher, and the curriculum. Yet the extent and range of differences may make it difficult for teachers to cope.

Some of the challenges of a diverse student body are subtle and go unrecognized. Children with backgrounds that are racially, linguistically, or culturally different from their teachers' may experience discontinuities in values between home and school or may lose self-esteem as they see little of their own history and culture represented and taught in the curriculum. Teachers may not be knowledgeable about the culture, values, expectations, and histories of each of the children in their classes. Sometimes students' learning is disrupted by these discontinuities, yet teachers are not aware of the role their expectations, values, or methods played in the student's failure. Locust (1988), for example, explains how common academic practices discriminate against and "wound the spirit" of Native American children. Several investigators have pointed to the overrepresentation of African-American and Latino children in the lowest academic tracks and in the population of children who drop out of school as a consequence of unresponsiveness to their learning needs.

Sometimes, differences in values are so profound that teachers find it difficult to accept or like certain students. One teacher with whom I spoke, for example, mentioned the emotional turmoil created in her by a boy in her class from a Middle Eastern country. His culture taught him not to accept the authority of a woman over his behavior and learning. She experienced the boy's dismissal of her interventions as threatening, confusing, and infuriating, yet recognized her obligation to help him learn. As a professor in a college that prepares many teachers, I see clearly that one of our great challenges is to help future teachers to recognize, understand, and find ways of respectfully resolving powerful value clashes that may emerge among themselves, the children they will teach, and the children's families.

The diversity of our children has outstripped the diversity of the teaching force. There is a chronic nationwide shortage of bilingual teachers. Moreover, only 11% of the country's teachers are people of color, and if current trends continue, the result will be a national teaching force that is 5% nonwhite serving a student population that is about 33% nonwhite (Hawley, 1989). As Hawley explains, these trends have two important negative consequences. The absence of interactions with successful teachers and administrators from nonwhite groups yields a dearth of role models for nonwhite children and contributes to racism and segregation in our society as a whole. In addition, when the teaching force is not multicultural, educators have fewer resources on which to draw for understanding and appreciating children's differences and the implications of those differences for teaching and learning.

SCHOOL NORMS THAT DO NOT SUPPORT PARTNERSHIP

Collaboration Among Adults—A Rarity

Adult collaboration in any form is relatively rare in schools. Collaboration is not the dominant model for the management of schools or the practice of teaching. The traditional approach to managing schools emphasizes hierarchy, individualism, and technology rather than dialogue, relationship, and reciprocity (see Noddings, 1988). And as Kidder (1989) has illustrated so compellingly in *Among School Children*, teaching has been and continues to be an isolated and isolating experience. Team teaching, collaborative problem solving, and a strong teachers' voice in school-based management are still the exception rather than the rule in America's schools.

Institutions that prepare teachers have done little to change the existing regularities in schools. Teacher preparation programs rarely emphasize a curriculum that would help teachers to find and use their own voices; to learn skills of working in groups of teachers or parents (such as decision making, conflict resolution, and collaborative problem solving); to understand the effects of different approaches to school management; or to explore the contributions of other human service professionals to family and community development. In short, since most schools are and have been hierarchically rather than collaboratively organized and managed, and our professional preparation institutions continue to prepare teachers for this model, it is not surprising that hierarchical and authoritarian principles govern the schools' relationships with parents as well.

Seeley (1985) sees this system of managing schools as fundamentally flawed.

> The essential trouble is the nature of the system itself, a system that has become beguiled by a "delivery system" mentality. Public education today is a professionalized, bureaucratized, governmental enterprise attempting to deliver education as a service. The system is faulty because it is designed to deliver something that cannot be delivered. The system is failing and will continue to fail until education is rediscovered as a dimension of human development dependent on personal motivation, initiative, and relationships, not on systems and "service delivery." (p. 4)

The school-based norm of individualism affects home–school relationships. Strong connections between parents and educators would run contrary to the normative value of individual self-sufficiency and the dominant practice of administrative decision making and delegation.

Seeley (1989) would concur, arguing that American schools have adopted a "delegation model" of parent involvement, where parents signal that they do not have to be involved because the job of education has been delegated to the schools, and educators see parent involvement as an interference with the jobs that have been delegated to them. In a delegation model, conversation is necessary only during crises. If schools are not doing their jobs, then parents (usually through the school committee) can replace unsatisfactory administrators with new ones, who would then resume responsibility for educating children.

Avoiding Conflict

Krasnow (1990a) emphasizes that one of the reasons that schools have failed to improve as organizations is that they have failed to learn how to deal constructively with conflict. She explains that, characteristically, interpersonal or intergroup conflict is not discussable in schools and negative information is withheld to avoid conflict.

In most school systems, administrators are rewarded for preserving the status quo, with collusion from the community about the sacredness of familiar traditions and practices. Thus, situations that are likely to result in conflict, even if that conflict may be seen by some as creative and growth-producing, have generally been avoided by school personnel.

Potential home–school partnerships are affected by the norm of avoiding conflict. Because, as I will argue, parents inevitably introduce conflict into the schools and thereby create distress and defensiveness, schools have developed over time a range of ritualized strategies that lessen both contact and conflict.

Although as educators we sometimes harken back to the "good old days" when home–school relationships were presumably stronger and more reliable, Sara Lawrence Lightfoot (1978) argues that the history of home–school relationships reveals a pattern of conflict extending from colonial times to the present that has caused these two systems to be "worlds apart." She explains:

> Families and schools are engaged in a complementary sociocultural task and yet they find themselves in great conflict with one another. One would expect that parents and teachers would be natural allies, but social scientists and our own experience recognize their adversarial relationship—one that emerges out of their roles as they are defined by the social structure of society, not necessarily or primarily the dynamics of interpersonal behaviors. (p. 20)

Lightfoot's conclusion about the inevitability of conflict emerges from an analysis of the different relationships that parents and educators have with children. The parents' focus is on the needs and interests of their own child, while teachers (and other school personnel) must attend to the needs of many children. Parents strive for the best possible education for their child, while educators must seek balance in distributing limited resources to many. A child's relationship with parents is more intense and intimate than with the teacher. Typically, a teacher focuses on growth in children's development of academic and socialization skills guided by objective national or local standards, while a parent is more concerned about a child's inner feelings and self-esteem.

Lightfoot generally sees these role differences as normative and potentially functional to the growth of children. However, she also asserts that if the expected conflict is intensified by asymmetries in status and power, or "when we perceive the origins of conflict as being rooted in inequality, ethnocentrism, or racism" (p. 41), then dysfunctional relationships of hostility and threat may result.

But as we have seen, school norms of conflict management prompt educators to view even role-based conflict as threatening and unpleasant, a strong signal of irreconcilable differences, and a rationale for keeping one's distance. All of the natural, structural differences mentioned above may be interpreted as the parents' failure to appreciate the educators' position. There is a tendency to see the conflict in personal terms, as evidence of the parents' inability to listen, understand, or care. When differences in background, culture, class, or power conspire to further distort the interpretation of verbal and nonverbal cues and the meaning of the dialogue, the discomfort and frustration are intensified.

Schools throughout the country have developed useful ways of avoiding conflict by bringing parents and teachers together in brief, ritualized encounters. As Lightfoot (1978) explains:

> Schools organize public, ritualistic occasions that do not allow for real contact, negotiation, or criticism between parents and teachers. Rather, they are institutionalized ways of establishing boundaries between insiders (teachers) and interlopers (parents) under the guise of polite conversation and mature cooperation. Parent-Teacher Association meetings and open house rituals at the beginning of the school year are contrived occasions that symbolically affirm the idealized parent–school relationship but rarely provide the chance for authentic interaction. (pp. 27–28)

My most recent experience as a parent of school-aged children confirms Lightfoot's point. At an open house at my daughter's middle school, the format was to proceed to each of her eight classes, where about 10 minutes were allocated for each teacher to explain his or her goals for the year. Just so there would be no confusion about the purpose of the evening, the principal announced over the loudspeaker during the "first period" that the evening was not designed as an opportunity for parents to speak individually with teachers about their youngsters. Individual conferences would need to be scheduled for another time. A legitimate request: Yet no teacher shared a telephone number, indicated an interest in a private conference, suggested a good time to be contacted at school, or otherwise demonstrated any interest in speaking more fully or authentically with parents at a future occasion.

I came away feeling grateful at having linked the faces with the names my daughter had been mentioning, and somewhat enlightened about the content of the year's curriculum. But I also felt disappointed at the lack of any personal connection; vaguely frustrated at having no idea of how my daughter was doing in this big, new school; impressed with being so carefully managed; and unsure about how or whether to pursue my interest in learning about my child's adjustment to a new school in the absence of any clear crisis.

And how was it for the teachers? They saw between 20 and 50 parents every 10 minutes. Despite the principal's careful directions about parent roles, some parents demanded their attention during the 3-minute transitions between classes. Most teachers were just beginning to warm up to their topic when the bell rang signaling the change of classes. If they did need or want to speak to a particular child's parents, there was no discreet way to do so. I imagine that for the teachers, too, the evening was vaguely frustrating, leading to questions about what they had conveyed about their curriculum and how or whether any further communication with parents should be sought.

The weight of tradition makes it very difficult to question the value of these activities. In one common prototype, parent–teacher conferences are mandated for children in elementary school. Parents arrive at 15-minute intervals over a 3-day period to discuss their children's growth. The conferences do allow parents and teacher to meet and share a sample of the child's work. They have symbolic importance, reflecting the mutual commitment of both parties to the education of the child, a connection that parents and educators value highly. These events maintain continuity and tradition.

But they do not permit authentic dialogue and effective problem solving. In what other circumstance would one allow only 15 minutes to share a significant amount of information about a situation of deep mutual concern with a virtual stranger? The press to play a symbolic role (perfect teacher, perfect parent) leads both parties to feel on display and to smooth over problems, limit honest dialogue, inhibit future connections, see themselves as separate, and experience vague or serious disappointment at the encounter, depending on goals and expectations.

Henderson's (1987) review of the literature and her own experience in schools highlight the standard practice of avoiding outreach to parents. Here she summarizes the most common reasons educators give for maintaining the separation between home and school.

> It is still not unusual to hear experienced educators say that once children are in school, their education is best left to the professionals—that untrained parents may unwittingly interfere with today's sophisticated teaching techniques, or even that turf battles between parents and teachers might disrupt the learning environment. They also argue that the extra time it takes to work with parents would place an intolerable burden on already overworked teachers and principals. (p. 2)

When parents do become involved in the school, particularly as a result of a concern, they are often perceived as threatening to the status or competence of educators. When parent involvement is sought, then, it is often within carefully circumscribed boundaries, as this teacher explained when describing desirable parent involvement.

> First an educated parent body, informed about goals for their children in school. From goals come questions, and then we should hold workshops for parents so they can be aware of what we are teaching and how we teach and the results we expect. Third, we need their support. We are a team. They need to be a part of their children's education. That doesn't mean they sit in the class, but by being supportive at home, their involvement is very important. (Swap, 1990a, p. 11)

In summary, schools as they are traditionally managed do not seek or support parent involvement that is based on equal relationships, collaborative problem solving, regular self-evaluation, or open discussion of conflict. The result is an unsatisfying cycle in which most conflict (even normal, useful conflict) is driven underground; the conflicts that do emerge tend to be explosive, threatening, and personalized; and the aftermath of these explosions reinforces the need for ritualized management of home–school relations. Though honored by long tradition, this is a cycle and a system that is wasteful of energy, destructive of positive motivation, and ineffective in supporting children's growth.

Wasteful and destructive as this system is, it is very resistant to change. Joyce, Bennett, and Rolheiser-Bennett (1990) draw this conclusion after reviewing the research on transforming the work environment of the school.

> Reorienting school cultures toward collegial problem solving and study and incorporation of advances in research on curriculum and teaching has turned out to be very difficult. The reason has not been an absence of models. . . .
> The problem is less one of conception than implementation. The culture of the school has proved to be a very tough customer indeed. (p. 33)

From my perspective, the "school culture" barrier is a dual one. It is difficult, first of all, to place the problem of home–school relationships into a cultural context rather than a personal one. Because most of us have grown up with these norms and traditional practices and worked in institutions that perpetuate them, it is difficult to untangle ourselves and evaluate them objectively. If we manage to break through that barrier, then implementation requires a radical revisioning of the school environment. As Seeley (1989) suggests, "We are confronted, then, with the need to discover and implement new policies and practices, as well as to change basic structures, roles, relationships, attitudes, and assumptions" (p. 46). Clearly, this is no trivial barrier to home–school partnerships.

LIMITED RESOURCES TO SUPPORT PARENT INVOLVEMENT

In a workshop that I offered to teachers recently, I asked them to identify the issues and constraints that kept them from reaching out to parents. One of the teachers replied without hesitation: "time and money." Although the allocation of time and money are also important components of school culture, I feel that they are so important in the context of home–school partnerships that they deserve their own category.

Time Allocated for Crises But Not for Building Relationships

Time is one of the most important resources in a school, and almost all of it is allocated to direct teaching. A regularity of school life is that in most systems, the importance of collaborative planning for the continual improvement of schools is not acknowledged and honored by the creation of a schedule that supports regular, frequent, and compensated meetings of adults. In keeping with this model, outreach to parents is seldom supported by the allocation of scheduled, compensated time. An administrator at the workshop said, "If it's important, then they'll give it time—real time, not just voluntary add-on." Finding real time continues to be a barrier to home–school partnerships.

As we have seen, changing demographics have made time even more precious and fragmented for both parents and educators. This reality needs to be acknowledged, accepted, and planned for; but usually it is not. Instead, parents and teachers often interpret the other's lack of availability as a signal of lack of concern for the child. We see missed connections in personal terms: Teachers chafe when parents fail to appear for conferences or neglect to carry out agreed-on educational activities at home. Parents despair when teachers talk to them only in 15-minute conferences and fail to recognize their child's special strengths. Anger and disappointment, frustration and exhaustion are commonplace.

In this struggle, we often see the other as at fault. Parents (especially mothers) and teachers (especially women) are supposed to be infinitely responsive, nurturant, freely giving, available, and focused on children. Parents and teachers convey to each other impossibly high expectations about their performance, and each group embodies for the other its disappointed expectations about perfection.

However, parents and teachers *do* make time for each other during a crisis. But at that point, the stage is set for trouble, and the time spent together is often punishing and adversarial. When trust, respect, and openness do not already exist in relationships between parents and teachers, it is difficult to build them in a crisis atmosphere.

A crisis elicits many complex emotions: sadness and disappointment that the child is not doing better; anger that the "other" adult could not prevent or fix it; secret worry about how our own incompetence as teachers or parents may have contributed to the problem; concerns about what others (relatives, neighbors, colleagues, principals) will think or say about the problem; perhaps even denial that a serious problem exists. Into this cauldron of important emotions must be added aspects of our own personal history: our experiences with past crises, current levels of stress from other sources, the length of our history with this child and its meaning to us. In crises we often anticipate negative, unrewarding, punishing interactions, which can become self-fulfilling prophecies. Communicating during a crisis is not impossible. But certainly the allocation of time to establish informal, trusting relationships between parents and teachers before a crisis emerges is a first step in collaborating effectively when a serious problem does occur.

Money Not Easily Allocated to Partnership Programs

In many states, the financial resources that are available to schools are declining. Most schools have chosen to concentrate the revenues that remain in essential personnel, programs, and supplies. These decisions make it difficult to initiate or maintain outreach programs for parents. Looked at in another way, such decisions also signal that schools do not consider home–school partnership essential to their mission. The lack of availability of money for start-up or expansion of partnership activities is a psychological and practical barrier to successful outreach.

Debate about how to reduce public spending is ongoing. In many communities, there is intense controversy about allocations in cities and towns. School budgets are subjected to continual scrutiny; school administrators' decisions are consistently criticized; and debate about the usefulness of music or language or special education budgets are publicly and personally debated. Often, many of the leaders on both sides of the debate are parents. In many communities, educators find the controversies themselves and their outcomes unsupportive and critical. In this charged atmosphere, and especially when parents are seen as disrespectful of educators or focused only on family interests, the motivation for collaboration with parents is sharply reduced.

LACK OF INFORMATION ABOUT
HOW TO ESTABLISH PARTNERSHIPS

In a survey of 3,700 elementary teachers in 600 schools, Epstein and Becker (1982) found that although most teachers agreed that parent involvement contributed to student achievement, they also reported not knowing how to establish parent involvement programs. Moreover, they had reservations about whether they could motivate parents to come to meetings or work with their children on learning activities at home.

Epstein (1985) argues that relatively few teachers make frequent or systematic use of parent involvement activities, in part because preservice and in-service training currently "results in attitudes and practices designed to keep parents out of the learning process and even out of the classroom" (p. 23). She explains that few institutions that prepare teachers offer required courses in parent involvement, and argues that teachers need educational programs that would teach them about the problems and potential of parent involvement; instruct them in designing, implementing, and evaluating practices for their own classroom; and expose them to existing materials and practices that work.

Epstein (1987) also points out that while administrative leadership in supporting parent involvement is very important in achieving good results, administrators often leave the selection and use of parent involvement activities to their teaching and support staff. She explains that "this lack of active administrative leadership and attention is due, in part, to the dearth of useful, organized information on parent involvement in schools" (p. 120).

In my experience, in-service education offered to principals or teachers on parent involvement is generally restricted to a single session—hardly enough time to confront complex attitudes, identify and work on needed skills, or learn about promising practices in other settings. Thus, although the information about the benefits of home–school partnership is easily accessible and often mentioned in professional journals, useful, organized information or comprehensive training that would help educators to incorporate the information into their own practice have not been widely available. Clearly, a fourth barrier to successful parent involvement programs is inadequate information and training.

BARRIERS FROM THE PARENTS' PERSPECTIVE

There is no question that changing demographics have made it more difficult for many families to participate in activities at school during the day. Parents will come to school activities, but with time so precious, they want to make sure that they are not wasting their time on activities where their involvement is not really wanted or valued, where their "second-class" status is underlined, or where they are not making a contribution to their child.

Increased diversity among the parent population and a sense of being different from school personnel may lessen parents' comfort in seeking contact with teachers or administrators. It is the perception of many Asian immigrant parents, for example, that communication with teachers is considered to be "checking up on them" and an expression of disrespect (Yao, 1988). These parents maintain the tradition of delegation and do not understand that their presence in school or in school-based activities is appropriate.

Finally, although the research of Davies (1988) and Epstein (1990) is unequivocal in concluding that almost all parents from all backgrounds care about the education of their children at school, those authors also explain that parents often do not know what is expected of them or how they might contribute to their child's schooling. Some parents respond to this confusion by withdrawing; others become angry and frustrated when the school seems to be failing to meet the needs of their youngster. Despite the problems, there is much goodwill, hope, and optimism among parents, particularly when their children are young, about the importance of schooling. This optimism can provide energy for collaboration.

SUMMARY

When the level of family involvement in schools is low despite its proven benefits, we must try to understand the barriers that inhibit reaching out to families. The problems in achieving partnerships between home and school have a long history. They are not primarily due to lack of concern or skill among either parents or teachers. Rather, they seem to arise from traditions within the school culture of running schools according to a hierarchical, noncollaborative, delegation model; avoiding conflict; utilizing ritualized formats that inhibit authentic communication; and failing to allocate sufficient resources of time and money to home–school relationships.

Difficulties in fostering home–school connections have been intensified in the last 2 decades by demographic changes. Changes in family structures, more mothers in the work force, higher rates of poverty, a growing discrepancy between the backgrounds of children and the teaching force, and historically high rates of immigration have made it more difficult for parents and teachers to find time for each other and to build open, trusting relationships. Discussion of important issues is thus often postponed until a crisis emerges. And it is, of course, most difficult to forge a partnership during a crisis, when emotions are strong, time is short, issues are complex, and solutions are not simple.

Teachers, parents, and administrators have generally received limited information about how to work together effectively. Information about creating effective parent involvement programs is rarely incorporated in preservice professional preparation programs, and in-service programs tend to be single-session experiences with no opportunity for supervised trial in schools. Parents consistently report an interest in supporting their children's learning, but are not clear about the school's expectations and are confused about how they can help.

Once understood, these barriers to home–school collaboration can be overcome. The remainder of this book will explain how.

CHAPTER 3

Three Models of
Home–School Relationships

Most of the teacher training and professional literature about improving home–school relationships has focused on improving teachers' or parents' interpersonal skills. The idea is that if individuals can learn to listen better or resolve conflicts more productively, then the school's relationships with parents will improve. Moreover, when parents or educators are asked to talk about how to improve home–school relationships, particular individuals pop into their minds. Parents will describe their children's current teachers. Teachers or principals will often describe a difficult conference (or prolonged interaction) with a particular parent. The focus of attention in understanding home–school relationships generally seems to be on individuals.

Yet a focus on individual interactions, though useful, does not get to the heart of improving home–school relationships. For example, teachers can attend an in-service workshop on listening skills, but whether they feel a commitment to learn these skills or maintain the motivation to use them generally depends on the norms that govern how the school works with parents. Whether or not individual teachers reach out to parents of children in their classrooms is dictated by policy (written or unwritten), custom, or culture as much as or more than by their individual inclinations. In fact, norms can countervene an individual's wishes. For example, I often hear teachers say, "I know what I would like to do, but my hands are tied." Or a principal will say, "I know that certain questions on that family information form really bother some parents, but the district office says we have to have one on file for every family."

When norms become organized in such a way that they govern the nature of home–school relationships and shape the hundreds of interactions that occur between parents and educators in a school, then this organized system of norms can be called a model. Models may be formal or informal, explicit or implicit, recognized or unrecognized, but they provide a consistent pattern of assumptions, goals, attitudes, behaviors, and strategies that help us to understand parent–educator relationships in that school.

Thinking about home–school relationships in terms of models is a new insight for me, the product of working in many schools across the country. I have come to believe that there are four models that describe relationships between parents and educators, each of which is defined by a different set of goals, assumptions, attitudes, behaviors, and strategies.

In this chapter, three models of home–school relationships will be presented: the Protective model (introduced in the last chapter, now with a label attached), the School-to-Home Transmission model, and the Curriculum Enrichment model. The Partnership model will be described in Chapter 4. Each of these models is in use in schools, and each has advantages and disadvantages, which will be outlined.

Developing an understanding of alternative models of home–school relationships can be useful. When we are members of a culture, it is difficult to see its dimensions and its power, or to distinguish between what is inevitable and what is within our power to change. Recognizing that there are several different models for adult collaboration and for home–school relationships is the first step in evaluating one's own system and developing a vision of change. Moreover, realizing that there are different approaches to parent involvement can stimulate debate among the faculty about the most appropriate goals and assumptions for a parent involvement program and help avoid the random, scatter-shot programming for parents that is characteristic of many schools. The description of the models that follows offers my best effort at clarifying the prototypes or blueprints for parent involvement that I have seen in operation in schools.

THE PROTECTIVE MODEL

Already described in Chapter 2 as the dominant model for home–school relationships, the goal of the Protective model is to reduce conflict between parents and educators, primarily through the separation of parents' and educators' functions. I have called it the Protective model because its aim is to protect the school from interference by parents. This model is driven by three assumptions.

1. Parents delegate to the school the responsibility of educating their children.
2. Parents hold school personnel accountable for the results.
3. Educators accept this delegation of responsibility.

Thus, parent involvement in decision making or collaborative problem solving would be seen as inappropriate and an interference with the educator's job.

Many teachers share this attitude. Here are two examples of teachers expressing this viewpoint when they were interviewed by other teachers from the Schools Reaching Out project (see Krasnow, 1990b) about their vision of desirable parent involvement.

> Parents should adhere to the rules and trust teachers to do what is right by their children. They should trust the fact that the teachers are following the program.

> Parents should be actively involved with students at home. The responsibility of parents ends at home. Teachers are responsible for teaching.

As we have seen, the strategies for parent involvement that emerge from such a vision are ones where ritualized formats dominate (such as the traditional open house) and in which opportunities for authentic dialogue are restricted.

The single advantage of this model is that it is generally very effective at achieving its goal of protecting the school against parental intrusion in most circumstances. The disadvantages are that it

- Exacerbates many conflicts between home and school by creating no structures or predictable opportunities for preventive problem solving
- Ignores the potential of home–school collaboration for improving student achievement
- Rejects rich resources for enrichment and school support available from families and other members of the community that could be available to the school.

THE SCHOOL-TO-HOME TRANSMISSION MODEL

Goals and Assumptions

The goal of this model is to enlist parents in supporting the objectives of the school. Its assumptions are that

- Children's achievement is fostered by continuity of expectations and values between home and school
- School personnel should identify the values and practices outside school that contribute to school success
- Parents should endorse the importance of schooling, reinforce school expectations at home, provide conditions at home that nurture development and support school success, and ensure that the child meets minimum academic and social requirements.

Most schools' parent involvement programs are based on this model. In contrast to the Protective model, the School-to-Home Transmission model acknowledges the continuous interchange between home and school and the important role that parents play in enhancing the educational achievement of their children. Epstein (1987) summarizes this viewpoint succinctly.

> The evidence is clear that parental encouragement, activities, and interest at home and participation in schools and classrooms affect children's achievements, attitudes, and aspirations, even after student ability and family socioeconomic status are taken into account. Students gain in personal and academic development if their families emphasize schooling, let the children know they do, and do so continually over the school years. (p. 120)

Parents have the important responsibility of helping their children succeed within the guidelines established by the school culture. Their role includes preparing their children to begin school, encouraging them to succeed in school, and transmitting values, attitudes, and skills that characterize those who succeed.

Many schools also rely on the presence of parents in school to support individual and group work, to contribute to the enrichment of the curriculum, and to facilitate a myriad of activities (preparing food for school parties, raising money, chaperoning at dances, cataloguing books for the library, preparing materials for teachers, building playgrounds). Parents may be involved on advisory boards or on decision-making committees, but if the program is operating according to a School-to-Home Transmission model, their numbers are proportionately small, and they are expected to play a supportive and subordinate role.

Within the School-to-Home Transmission model, it is school personnel who define goals and programs. Two-way communication is not sought because the goal is for parents to understand and support the school's objectives. That focus is clear in the words of a teacher interviewed in an urban school, who illustrated many of the assumptions of the School-to-Home Transmission model when she explained her concept of desirable parent involvement.

> Parents should be trained to parent, talk to their kids more—interact with children and take them places. [By desirable parent involvement, I mean] parents cooperating with homework, looking at it, reading notices, coming to school when called, taking an interest in their children's education.

A Closer Look at What Schools Transmit. The question of what skills, values, and attitudes schools transmit to homes is a very complex one. As we have seen, schools are very powerful cultures. They define the conditions under which schooling can take place and the criteria for youngsters' success. They also embody assumptions and values that predominate in the social, political, and economic structures of the larger society. Comer (1980) terms this predominant view in American culture the "social mainstream" and links student success in school to acquisition of the values and skills that characterize this perspective.

> Children whose parents feel that they can and should be a part of the social mainstream have the best chance to acquire the social skills that will lead to school and life success. Children whose parents are not a part of the social mainstream can acquire such skills if they are taught in school and if there is parental support for their acquisition and use. (p. 192)

Access to the Social Mainstream. Comer (1988c) explains the difficulties that occur when children have not acquired this background and are not ready to take advantage of traditional schooling.

> American education is structured to serve children who have had the average family experience or better. Teachers are not trained to work with children who have not had such an experience. In the selection of teachers little attention is given to their ability to work with other than mainstream children. . . . Children who have not been read to, helped to learn how to think, express themselves, and don't show good problem-solving competence and confidence are often viewed as slow, with limited academic achievement potential. (p. 215)

Comer's solution is to teach children the skills they need to succeed in mainstream society. But many educators and historians have contended that members of the social mainstream have not made it easy for those who are not privileged to enter this circle. They argue that schools become agents of the dominant culture's exclusiveness by blaming children's families for their lack of preparation, lowering expectations for children from these groups, and not making the desirable norms for behavior explicit. A corollary issue is that strengths, values, and skills that children from nonmainstream backgrounds bring to school that are different from the dominant culture may go unnoticed or unappreciated (see Delpit, 1988; Hidalgo, 1992; Perry, 1992; Siu, 1992; Swap & Krasnow, 1992).

The desire of parents from traditionally oppressed cultures to provide access to success for their children through education has been very carefully documented, though it does not seem to be widely known. For example, in a history of education of blacks in the South from 1860 to 1935, Anderson's (1988) research revealed that throughout the slave community there was "a fundamental belief in learning and self-improvement and a shared belief in universal education as a necessary basis for freedom and citizenship" (p. 281). This belief was manifested in many ways, but perhaps most dramatically in the hundreds of secret schools that slaves established despite the prohibition against literacy for slaves, and later in the heroic efforts that were made by blacks in many parts of the South after the Civil War to raise funds to build a common school system to provide access to education for all their children.

Nonetheless, for the majority of black children in the South between 1860 and 1935, even education at the elementary level was not available. Anderson concludes: "The education of blacks in the South reveals that various contending forces sought either to repress the development of black education or to shape it in ways that contradicted blacks' interests in intellectual development" (p. 285). He finds it ironic that given a long history in which the opportunities to gain access to education were appallingly difficult, "a body of historical and social science literature was built up which tended to interpret blacks' relatively lower levels of educational attainment in the twentieth century as the product of initial differences in attitude or cultural orientation toward learning and social improvement" (p. 285).

Delpit (1988) contends that schools today are continuing to deny certain children access to the social mainstream because schools do not make clear and then teach the codes or rules for participating in "the culture of power" that are essential for success in school. These rules include the preferred linguistic forms, communicative strategies, and means for presenting oneself. The need to teach these skills is not generally obvious to school personnel, Delpit maintains, because "those with power are frequently least aware of—or least willing to acknowledge its existence" (p. 282). For example, if a child is used to direct commands ("Put the scissors on the shelf"), then an indirect command ("Is this where the scissors belong?") delivered in a soft-spoken, nonassertive tone will not carry the same message to the child. When the child responds inappropriately (e.g., "I guess so" or even "Yes ma'am"), the teacher may feel that the child is rude, noncompliant, unobservant, or slow. If the teacher acts on any of these perceptions, then the child is likely to feel misunderstood and unsupported. Thus, a negative dance can begin, not because of any lack of eagerness from either partner, but because each has learned different steps for the dance—and neither is aware that this is the case.

One solution to this problem is for parents who are not members of the school mainstream to learn the "rules" for success and convey them to their children. This is what happened during James Comer's childhood, for example. Comer is an African-American man, now a prominent child psychiatrist and educator, who has devoted much of his energy in the last 3 decades to creating schools where true home–school partnership occurs. He credits his mother, however, with teaching him the skills that allowed him to succeed in schools where the majority of children were white and middle class.

As he explains in *Maggie's American Dream* (1988c), his great grandmother was a slave, and his mother was a domestic with almost no formal education. Yet his mother supported his achievement by going to school functions, advocating for him with teachers, insisting on fine work, and taking him to the library. She learned the lexicon of how to be an effective parent and what it took for a black child to be successful in predominantly white schools by carefully listening to the white women for whom she worked. She said: "So many people would just work and pay no attention to what's going on. I didn't just cook and clean. I worked with my eyes and ears open. I watched and listened to them and the way they lived. For me it was like going to school" (p. 60).

School personnel recognize that parents are not always successful in preparing their children to learn in schools as they are currently constituted. In these circumstances, educators may either simply accept this situation or elect to offer training to parents, children, or both. Offering training to parents is at the heart of the School-to-Home Transmission model, and, as we have seen, many of these efforts result in increased success for children at school.

A Deficit Approach. However, when schools offer training and parents do not participate or follow through, school personnel often feel that their concerns about parents' deficiencies are confirmed. But often these conclusions are overgeneralized. The deficit approach to family involvement, particularly for poor families, is very widespread, as this excerpt from a paper on parent involvement released by the U.S. Department of Education as part of its "Policy Perspectives" series reveals.

> The effective functioning of schools has depended on the effective function-
> ing of the family and community. What makes some ghetto schools function
> poorly is that the communities and families they serve are weak, lacking the
> social capital that would reinforce the school's goals. (Coleman, 1991, p. 13)

Referring to families and whole communities as "weak," ineffective in
their functioning, lacking in social capital, and contributing to poor functioning in schools ignores differentiated patterns of weakness and strength
in urban communities and blames families for ineffective schools.

In the following quote, a teacher describes how her deficit orientation toward parents changed based on a home visit to a parent of a child
in her classroom:

> I began to understand how societal pressures were intertwined with the
> mission of the school. Educators must be sensitive to these variables and
> refrain from quick decisions. I had adopted the stereotype that Blacks living
> in ghetto areas did not care about schooling. The stereotypes I had acquired
> contributed to my ineffectiveness as a teacher. I chose the indulgent belief
> that the problem was in the student and that I had done all I could do.
>
> This experience [making a visit to the home of an African-American
> child who was often absent from school] helped me develop a multidimen-
> sional understanding of the achievement concerns facing Black American
> parents. For many poor Black parents, education is crucial because there is
> more at stake than grades. They expect schools to teach their children the
> skills that will empower them to transcend poverty. Because of this urgent
> desire for their children to succeed, Black parents may feel severe frustration
> if their children have continually failed in school. Ambivalent feelings can
> make them distrustful. Jimmy's mother wanted him to do well, but she felt
> the school represented a hostile institution. It was important to open lines of
> communication with her so she felt ownership in the educational process.
> (Pang, 1988, p. 377)

Although there is no question that there are a small percentage of
families that are dysfunctional, most families who do not participate in
school do not fall into this category. Yet we rarely question the effectiveness of our outreach strategies or seek advice from parents about the kind
of information or support they would find helpful. It is even more rare to
offer the kind of training that Delpit would see as most helpful to parents;
that is, training that acknowledges the existence of alternative world
views and cultures and that provides explicit, nonjudgmental guidelines
for parents that would help them and their children to learn about the
culture of power. (A more radical alternative is to change the ways in
which schools are currently constituted to embrace a more democratic,

multicultural perspective—but this approach is the focus of the Interactive and True Partnership models, to be discussed shortly.)

Strategies for Parent Involvement

Within the School-to-Home Transmission model, educators have a responsibility to communicate with parents in order to inform them about their children's progress, school policies and programs, and opportunities for involvement. In two schools I visited, for example, newsletters sent home by the principal and teachers and a school visiting week were communication strategies that worked well. Schools often offer parent education workshops to support parents in carrying out their role. These might include lectures or seminars on topics such as stages of child development, love and discipline, listening to your child, or helping with homework. Some programs also offer courses or workshops on topics such as English as a Second Language, adult basic education, or job interviewing skills to help build parents' knowledge and skills in more generic ways (see Swap, 1990c, for examples of activities offered by two schools).

Schools might develop volunteer programs to involve parents in school or pay parents to work as aides in classrooms. To ensure continuity of learning between home and school, teachers might prepare enrichment packets, use commercially available materials that supplement standard curriculum series, send homework explanation sheets home, or set up "homework hotlines" for parents who have questions about homework. Many schools develop simple and effective home reading programs (Epstein, 1987; Krasnow, 1990h) or bring students, family members, and teachers together to improve students' work; for example, through the Family Math Program (Lawrence Hall of Science, 1979). (Examples of additional strategies in each of these areas will be presented in subsequent chapters.)

In summary, strategies that support parent involvement according to the School-to-Home Transmission model can generate important and useful connections in the areas of communication, support for parents, parent support for the school, and home learning.

Evaluation

Programs based on the School-to-Home Transmission model have been useful in increasing children's school success. Most of the programs reviewed in Chapter 1 were based on this model, where school personnel supported parents in working with their children at home according to specific guidelines. We have seen that parents seek clear direction from the school about the social and academic skills that are needed for children's success and about their role in supporting the development of those skills (Epstein, 1990). Thus, clear transmission of information can be a welcome offering to parents, particularly when they have not had access to the social mainstream and seek such access for their children. However, inherent in this philosophy are also four potential dangers.

1. Programs built on this model often contain components that reflect an unwillingness to consider parents as equal partners having important strengths. For example, relationships may be defined through a contract, and parents may be reinforced for meeting their obligations. Parents may or may not be consulted about what should be done at home (or at school) or how it should be done. Workshops or activities may be designed explicitly to help parents "be more effective" in their role, suggesting that school personnel know more than parents about how to parent and that parents may be considered deficient.

   In general, parents in a one-way communication model are not encouraged to express concerns or offer ideas and opinions. If parents feel that they are not respected or that they are blamed for their children's difficulties, they may hesitate to become involved or may become disillusioned over time.

2. All parents may not be able to devote sufficient time and energy to parent involvement activities if such conditions as dangerous housing, poor health, or stringent employment requirements interfere. If schools recognize these constraints and can provide a link to resources that would address them, then community programs, health and mental health services connected to the school, and neighborhood support groups can be safety nets for children and their families (see Heath & McLaughlin, 1987; Kagan, 1989). In an inner city school where I worked, for example, the parent center coordinator was very successful in linking some parents to the resources they needed to find housing, fuel assistance, and warm clothing. Only after these basic needs were met and their time-consuming bureaucratic requirements were satisfied, were parents ready to participate in the school.

   Mamie Johnson, the principal of P.S. 146 in New York City, who has been extremely effective in linking family, school, and community resources, explains her approach to families in need.

   > We need to look at schools as educational centers for the whole community, adults as well as kids. Many of our families are in deep crisis. If the resources to help them are more than four blocks away, they won't

use them. Parents automatically turn to the schools with their problems, but we don't always have the answer. We need to be family focused, and we need to find those agencies who have the expertise to deal with the families' needs. . . . We need to reach out not only to families but to other community-based organizations and see how they can become part of the school. (Clinchy, 1992, p. 33)

3. Using the School-to-Home Transmission model, schools may find it difficult to draw clear boundaries between the roles of school and home in formal education. In its most exaggerated form, parents would be asked to teach whatever skills their child was not acquiring, regardless of the financial or emotional costs to families. Moreover, parents might be blamed if their interventions did not result in higher student achievement.
4. A fourth concern is the danger of demeaning the value and importance of the family's culture in the effort to transmit the values and goals of the school. This concern becomes increasingly important as our teaching staff becomes more monocultural and our student body becomes more diverse.

The School-to-Home Transmission model has much to recommend it. For schools that have been organized and managed according to a delegation model, this model provides many opportunities for useful and pleasant home–school contact and for mutual effort to support students' success in school.

Since it maintains educators' control over parent programs and the degree to which parents are incorporated into the school, the School-to-Home Transmission model may provide a framework for the transition between a protective stance with parents and a more collaborative one. If the experiences of school personnel are positive over time and good relationships are developed through sustained contact, school personnel's control of programs may give way to a more comfortable and mutual exchange of ideas and joint planning.

Schools reflect and perpetuate the dominant values and beliefs of the society they serve. Schools also offer the opportunity for those who have not been traditionally successful to "make it," generally by learning the rules and succeeding in the areas dictated by the dominant culture. These are principles that are reflected in the School-to-Home Transmission model. Educators who are using this approach have many choices to make about what information they should transmit and to whom. Those choices strongly influence the degree to which all of America's children can be successful.

THE CURRICULUM ENRICHMENT MODEL

Goals and Assumptions

The goal of the Curriculum Enrichment model is to expand and extend the school's curriculum by incorporating into it the contributions of families. The assumption is that families have important expertise to contribute and that the interaction between parents and school personnel and the implementation of the revised curriculum will enhance the educational objectives of the school. This orientation has emerged for two different reasons. One of these has been to make the school curriculum more accurately reflect the views, values, history, and learning styles of the families represented in the school, particularly those of immigrant minorities and castelike minorities (Ogbu's distinction, 1983, 1990). The logic that drives this effort at curriculum reform is that

1. Continuity of learning between home and school is of critical importance in encouraging children's learning.
2. The values and cultural histories of many children are omitted from the standard school curriculum, leading to a disruption of this continuity between home and school, and often to less motivation, status, and achievement for these children in school.
3. These omissions distort the curriculum, leading to a less accurate and less comprehensive understanding of events and achievements and to a perpetuation of damaging beliefs and attitudes about immigrant and oppressed minorities.

A second reason for parents to be involved in curriculum enrichment occurs when schools can improve their curriculum by drawing on the special expertise that parents may have to share by virtue of their education and background. Interaction between parents and school personnel can result in, for example, the installation of a computer lab, instruction for teachers in the use of computers in the classroom, the addition of mathematics or science curriculum that is more experience-based, the integration of the newest technology in a vocational training program, or instruction in music composition.

In each case, two important assumptions guide the interaction between parents and teachers.

1. Parents and educators should work together to enrich curriculum objectives and content.

2. Relationships between home and school are based on mutual respect, and both parents and teachers are seen as experts and resources in this process of discovery.

The Curriculum Enrichment model is different from the other models I discuss because its assumptions do not necessarily permeate all aspects of the school culture and structure: Its focus is on curriculum and instruction. Sometimes only certain classrooms or programs or subject areas within a school or district embrace this philosophy. Though this lack of consistency across all the models makes me uncomfortable, I have chosen to include the Curriculum Enrichment model because it represents a distinctive approach to home–school relationships that is well conceptualized and in use in many schools.

Moreover, the area of curriculum development has historically been one where parental intrusion has been actively resisted. For many educators, curriculum is seen as the centerpiece of their professional expertise. Some teachers believe that their experience and training are devalued by parent involvement in curriculum planning, and they worry that parental advocacy may lead to inappropriate curriculum selections (see Chapter 9 for a more extended discussion). Given these concerns about parent involvement in curriculum development, the effort that many schools are making to experiment with parental contributions to curriculum enrichment is particularly noteworthy.

Illustrations

Multicultural Curriculum. Recently, many schools have been adopting an interactive approach to curriculum development because their student population is becoming increasingly diverse (and their teaching force is not). As described in Chapter 2, the populations of children from both immigrant and historically oppressed minorities are increasing. Most schools are searching for resources in multicultural education. The curriculum transformation that is being sought is not a trivialized exploration of the artifacts, holidays, and foods of peoples from other cultures—an approach to multicultural education that a school board member in Los Angeles called "one food, two heroes and three holidays" (Goldberg quoted in First & Carrera, 1988, p. 52). Nor is the goal to supply information about other cultures as an afterthought or addendum to the standard curriculum. What is sought in many systems is a new, fully integrated curriculum that accurately represents histories, points of view, and achievements of immigrant and oppressed minorities.

A teacher captures the essence of the interactive model of mutual learning in this excerpt from an interview about parent involvement.

> It was part of the program to have parents in my class. It was good . . . they saw how things were done. They taught us a few things. There were different cultures, and they taught us their way of doing things and they learned from us. It is not a one-way thing. (Swap, 1990c, p. 27)

What follows are three illustrations of attempts to use parent expertise to create a new, culturally sensitive approach to teaching and learning.

In the context of a family literacy program, Auerbach (1989) offers a very clear conceptualization of the philosophy that undergirds the Curriculum Enrichment model. She explicitly rejects any home–school connection that sees immigrant parents as deficient because they are not at ease with formal schoolwork. Instead, she incorporates aspects of the home culture into the school's curriculum by including as part of the content of that curriculum a broad range of activities and practices from the fabric of the families' daily lives. As she explains:

> The analysis in this article points to a social-contextual model of family literacy that asks, How can we draw on parents' knowledge and experience to inform instruction? rather than How can we transfer school practices into home contexts? The goal then is to increase the social significance of literacy in family life by incorporating community cultural forms and social issues into the context of literacy activities. This model is built on the particular conditions, concerns, and cultural expertise of specific communities, and, as such, does not involve a predetermined curriculum or set of practices and activities. Instead, the curriculum development process is participatory and is based on community life. (p. 177)

Another example of a curriculum that draws on the "conditions, concerns, and cultural experience of families" is one that was initiated by Inupiat Eskimo parents in North Barrow, Alaska. These parents came to resist education for their children that reflected only Western values. Okakok (1989) explained that after local control of public schooling was granted to the natives in the mid-1970s, the community insisted that "although Western education would serve its purpose, it would now be a purpose determined by our own people" (p. 407). She continued:

> While seeking to produce students with academic achievements comparable to those of other areas of the United States, the Board has also sought to

bring into our schools certain elements of historical and contemporary Inupiat Eskimo culture and knowledge of our natural environment. We have found that the attainment of academic skills in our students is directly related to our ability to successfully introduce Inupiat Eskimo concepts and educational practices into our schools. (p. 408)

A third example emerged as part of a staff development program. Shirley Brice Heath (1983) was a teacher trainer in a school in the Carolina Piedmonts that served children from several communities, including two rural communities in which she conducted extensive ethnographic research. As I understand it, none of the teachers in the school came from these two communities. In a focused staff development effort, teachers reflected on the insights that Heath had gained during her observations, supplemented these observations with their own experiences in the classroom, and analyzed points of difference between the two rural cultures and their own. They also made explicit the implications for children's learning that emerged from the many differences they discovered in ways of learning, talking, living, and thinking.

Perhaps most important, they discovered new ways of teaching children from these communities. Heath provides an extended example of a first-grade teacher who, after participating in this staff development effort, chose to work exclusively with children from one of these communities. These children—black, working class, and rural—had already been labeled as "potential failures." By designing materials and instructional practices that reflected her new understanding of the children's "ways of knowing," she was able to support 18 of the 19 children in achieving success. By the end of the year, all but one were reading at least at first-grade level; six were at second-grade level; eight were at third-grade level.

Science Education. Working closely with parents whose professional expertise offers resources to the school is a growing phenomenon. As an example, I will describe a program in science education in the Torrey Pines School in La Jolla, California, which was initiated by two mothers with degrees in science and experience in teaching at local universities. These parents spoke to the principal about a program in another school called the "Integrated Curriculum Approach" that offered useful approaches to curriculum and instruction. The principal was intrigued and supported an active exploration of these new teaching approaches by inviting experts into the school who demonstrated some of the techniques, arranging for all the teachers to visit the school where the program was in use, and promoting active discussion of the ideas that were sparked by the visits.

The parents offered to develop learning centers in science, drawing on the volunteer help of other parents and grandparents to staff them. Initially the centers were set up in the library, but subsequently they were moved into classrooms on a rotating basis. Space exploration, animals, and natural history were themes chosen for the centers during the first year. Most teachers participated in exchange of ideas and information with parents, mutual planning, and integration of these themes into the ongoing curriculum.

When I observed a class that had just rotated into the natural science unit, the excitement of the children and adults was apparent. There were many opportunities for hands-on learning appropriate to different learning styles; science content was integrated into mathematics and literature activities; and I saw many examples of students drawing on their supervised experiences with live reptiles (snakes, turtles, lizards), to construct hypotheses, make comparisons, analyze differences, and write about their findings. Although the principal explained that the teachers were initially apprehensive about the idea of parents in their classrooms and parent involvement in curriculum, over the course of the year the experience opened up new pathways, enriched the curriculum, generated a lot of enthusiasm, and promoted useful and respectful interactions between parents and teachers.

Another unanticipated benefit was that the children who were bused into the school through the Voluntary Ethnic Enrichment Program (primarily Latino children) seemed to take special advantage of the learning opportunities offered in this enriched curriculum. Although it was not clear why, the presence of their parents and grandparents in the classroom and the multisensory, experimental approach were suggested as possible reasons.

Strategies for Implementation

In each of the multicultural illustrations described above, the culture and history of the students' families—Latino, Native American, African-American—were valued by school personnel and were integrated with classroom learning. The Latino and Native American families worked directly with educators to develop an integrated curriculum; in the case of Heath (1983), families provided information but were not directly involved in the staff development effort. (I would suggest that the direct interpersonal contact between parents and educators adds an important dimension and is most likely to yield other benefits for children and adults.)

There are several types of activities that schools or parents might initiate that would reflect the philosophy of this model. At the Ellis

School in Roxbury, Massachusetts, for example, teachers and parents worked together to develop community portraits as part of the social studies, writing, and arts curriculum. A majority of the children in the school are African-American. Goode (1990) explains how the community portrait activity worked in the fourth-grade class.

> [Each of the students read *The Secret of Gumbo Grove* by Eleanora Tate.] It is the story of a girl, around the age of the fourth graders, who learned about the history of her community by researching old church records and by exploring the local cemetery and unraveling some long-held secrets. The fourth grade students learned about obstacles that she encountered and how she overcame them. For a class project, these students are researching their family histories and some of their writings will be in the book by Ellis students. These fourth grade students invited me to their classroom, and (with another teacher trained in oral history techniques) we demonstrated how to do an interview. The students observed first, then exchanged places as interviewer and interviewee in order to play both parts. They responded to this enthusiastically. (pp. 35–36)

Another very important strategy that encourages interactive learning and curriculum enrichment is involving parents from the community as tutors, volunteers in the classroom, or paid professional aides. As the teacher quoted earlier in this section suggested, continual contact between parents and educators helps adults to learn how each "does things" and supports two-way learning. Lightfoot (1978) also explains how the presence of parents from the community transforms the curriculum and creates continuity between home and school for children.

> It is important to recognize that the presence of parents in the school not only provides more adults to teach reading or to offer help and support to children but also transforms the culture of the school. With these black mothers present, there is no way that the curriculum and environment could remain unchanged. Even if the content of the lesson appears the same on paper, the transmission of the lesson takes on a different quality and character when presented by the mothers. Even if the concepts are unfamiliar and alien to the child's experience, the mother-teacher's style of interaction, her face, and her character are not strange. It feels like home. (p. 173)

A teacher in another school integrates all of her curriculum around central themes such as an exploration of the culture and history of Japan or Haiti. Extensive research and using parents and other community members as resources and resident experts are part of her curriculum development process (Richards, 1993). In an urban school, the positive

results of incorporating multicultural curriculum into the classroom encouraged a subcommittee of teachers and parents to work together on
the idea of making the curriculum and context of the whole school
multicultural. The program they recommended was based on an explicit
philosophy that emphasized valuing each child's heritage, incorporating
it into the curriculum, and finding new strategies to reduce conflict in the
school. The program would include bringing families' language, culture,
and ethnicity into the school in positive ways, as well as child development and staff development activities.

There are also several strategies that schools could use to identify
and draw on parents' expertise in their areas of professional interest.
Questionnaires that provide the opportunity for parents to identify their
areas of special interest or expertise and to indicate their availability to
contribute may be an important first step. Follow-up calls to explore
possible fits between parents' backgrounds and priority areas for curriculum enrichment would be an appropriate next step. If a school community has established particular goals for school improvement (say, moving to a literature-based reading approach), then parental resources
connected to those areas could be specifically requested.

Evaluation

This model for interactive learning and the development of enriched
curriculum offers an attractive approach for incorporating parent involvement into children's learning. Drawing on the knowledge and expertise
of parents increases the resources available to the school and provides
rich opportunities for adults to learn from each other.

Within the Curriculum Enrichment model, the contributions of immigrant or oppressed minorities who have not traditionally participated
fully in schools are especially welcomed. The power of the model
emerges from the explicit recognition of strengths of families from many
different backgrounds and from the necessity of providing continuity in
concepts, values, and educational practices between home and school for
all the nation's children. As research in multicultural curriculum explodes,
there is also growing recognition that the insights gained provide an
important corrective to inaccurate or one-sided portrayals of events and
achievements in American and world history.

There are difficulties in implementing the model. When the focus is
multicultural education, there are three important constraints. First,
creating continuity between home and school demands a significant
investment of parents' and educators' time, resources, support, and study.
Time for parents and teachers to get together is always at a premium. In

the area of multicultural curriculum, moreover, it is a very difficult task even for motivated teachers and parents to tease out differences in cultural values and practices. Although an enormous amount of research and work is underway to revise inaccurate texts, publish neglected resources, and incorporate important contributions made by people of color into the curriculum (e.g., see Perry & Fraser, 1993), the task is far from complete, and appropriate curriculum resources are not easily available.

A second concern is that the number of different cultures represented in particular classrooms may make curricular adaption very complex. In one small elementary school I visited in California, parent meetings were held with four different "culture-like" groups (Caucasian, Latino, African-American, and Vietnamese) to ascertain each group's priorities and concerns related to their children's learning. Another California school has invested in headsets for use at parent meetings, so that parents who have come from several different countries are able to participate. Although this degree of diversity brings the need for school responsiveness to the forefront, obviously it also complicates the task of interactive learning and may lead to fragmentation of effort or trivialization of each culture's contributions.

Third, a debate still rages in this country about what the school's mission should be in educating children with diverse backgrounds. Is there a majority culture and should it be taught to all, or should the diversity of our children be reflected and valued in the curriculum? A full integration of the diverse contributions of children from many backgrounds really changes the conditions of schooling. It is a radical notion in our schools and a prelude to achieving a "new common culture, one that allows the histories, cultures, and traditions of the historically uppressed to critically inform the formation of new narratives and metaphors" (Perry, 1990, p. 9).

The intellectual task of transforming the curriculum to reflect different voices in our history is hard, but the psychological task may be still harder, as passions around "giving up" traditional ways of teaching and "watering down the curriculum" are easily activated. The philosophy of interactive learning precipitates this debate. Therefore, individuals' concerns both about the intellectual tasks of researching and presenting new curriculum and the psychological tasks of examining complex beliefs and feelings must be addressed in any successful effort at curriculum reform.

In the areas of both multicultural education and curriculum enrichment in academic and vocational areas, barriers to interaction and sharing need to be overcome. Differences in class or educational background can make teachers and parents feel uncomfortable and threatened, and turf concerns need to be addressed and negotiated.

SUMMARY

The models in use for parent involvement programs are not and cannot be neutral: Although the assumptions that underlie them are seldom made explicit, they compel predictable attitudes and practices.

The Protective model was identified as a blueprint for avoiding intensive interactions between home and school and for keeping the roles of parents and teachers separate. The School-to-Home Transmission model emphasizes the importance of continuity between home and school, but looks to educators to determine what information should be transmitted to the home and which parents should receive it. The Curriculum Enrichment model emphasizes the importance of continuity in learning between home and school and the utility of reciprocal interactions between parents and educators. Generally, however, the focus of these activities is restricted to the development of curriculum and instructional practices—the extension of this reciprocal dialogue into school improvement or school management is not part of the model. The advantages and disadvantages of each model were briefly outlined.

In Chapter 4, we will look at the fourth model for home–school relationships, the Partnership model, in which collaborative relationships between home and school permeate all areas of school culture.

CHAPTER 4

A New Vision:
The Partnership Model

Envision a school where children are working hard, succeeding academically, and feeling good about themselves; where teachers are working enthusiastically with each other, with administrators, and with other resource persons to figure out even better ways to reach all the children; where parents and grandparents are champions of the school and committed to working with educators toward a common mission; where community resources enrich the school's curriculum and provide support to the staff. This vision is being realized in some of our nation's schools, and this chapter is devoted to identifying some of the ideas and structures that have translated this vision into reality.

One key to implementing this vision is developing a new model of home–school relationships. Emerging as a response to the crisis in American education, the Partnership model describes an alliance between parents and educators to encourage better schools and the success of all children in school. In this book, partnership has a very specific meaning that encompasses long-term commitments, mutual respect, widespread involvement of families and educators in many levels of activities, and sharing of planning and decision-making responsibilities.

In this chapter, I will present the goals and assumptions of the Partnership model, case examples of schools in which this model has become a blueprint for action, and an evaluation of its advantages and disadvantages. At the conclusion of the chapter, I will outline the four primary components of a parent involvement program that is based on a Partnership model. These components will provide the framework for a detailed exploration of how to create an effective parent involvement program: the focus of the remainder of this book.

It is important to clarify that the four models of home–school relationships are not necessarily arranged in an ascending order of desirability. The model of choice depends on the values of families and educators and the needs of the children. In China, for example, the culture supports what I have termed the Protective model. Involvement is not expected by parents or educators; in fact, families' respect for educators is manifested through noninvolvement. Centuries of tradition, a consistent value orientation related to education, and a level of academic success for children that is satisfactory to families and educators maintain the importance of this model in that culture. In the South prior to integration, shared values and comfortable interpersonal relationships among African-American teachers and parents led to satisfaction with parent involvement that consisted primarily of family support of children's learning and community activities outside the school walls (Theresa Perry, personal communication, April 27, 1992).

Without suggesting that the Partnership model is desirable for all, I would argue that it is the model of choice when these conditions obtain: Most children are not doing well in school; the population of children and families is heterogeneous; and there is a lack of agreement among families and educators about the definition of success in school and the characteristics of children and schools that contribute to success. Embracing the Partnership model is not easy: It requires an investment of time and a shift of attitudes for many participants. The process requires training and certainly involves conflict. Yet in my opinion, this model and the collaborative, inquiry-based, results-driven approaches that form its philosophical underpinnings, offer our best hope for resolving the current crisis in American education.

When children are doing reasonably well in school, when the community provides the school with sufficient resources, and when teacher morale is high, there is less impetus to pursue the Partnership model. However in many communities, in suburban and rural areas as well as in urban centers, the economic recession has revealed a lessened community commitment to the importance of public education and a lack of consensus about what quality education means. Annual Gallup polls reveal that teacher morale is at a low ebb, yet the maturing teaching force that remains in the schools is seeking a more powerful role in reform and decision making. For educators in some of these sites, the Partnership model holds promise as a framework for a "new" commitment to the democratic hope of success for all, to the importance of strong relationships within the school and community, to a spirit of experimentation and inquiry that supports risk-taking as well as careful evaluation, and to a model that focuses on growth and building on strengths in adults as well as children.

GOALS AND ASSUMPTIONS

In the Partnership model, the primary goal is for parents and educators to work together to accomplish a common mission, generally, for all children in school to achieve success. There are two important assumptions.

1. Accomplishing the joint mission requires a re-visioning of the school environment and a need to discover new policies and practices, structures, roles, relationships, and attitudes in order to realize the vision.
2. Accomplishing the joint mission demands collaboration among parents, community representatives, and educators. Because the task is very challenging and requires many resources, none of these groups acting alone can accomplish it.

The language used to describe this philosophy is radical and visionary. For example, Seeley (1989) borrows Kuhn's term "paradigm shift" to capture the idea of a fundamental restructuring of attitudes toward home–school partnership. Hopfenberg, Levin, Meister, and Rogers (1990) use the terms "unity of purpose," "empowerment," and "building on strengths" to illustrate the principles behind the transformation of school practices and culture that they envision. The authors explain further:

"How can it be . . ." wonders Larry Cuban, "that so much school reform has taken place over the last century yet schooling appears to be pretty much the same as it has always been?" (Cuban, 1988). The answer to Cuban's question, and the key to eliciting lasting and meaningful change in schools, lies in the inextricable connection between educational practice and the school culture in which these practices come to life. Practices cannot change without deeper transformations in the attitudes, meanings, and beliefs of schooling. (p. 10)

There is a sense of urgency and energy in this vision, a conviction that time is running out as teacher morale sinks lower and more children are underachieving or dropping out of our schools. There is also a sense of optimism that this re-visioning will be the first step in creating school environments in which both adults and children learn, care, work together, and succeed.

The partnership philosophy differs from the School-to-Home Transmission model in its emphasis on two-way communication, parental strengths, and problem solving with parents. It differs from the Curriculum Enrichment model in promoting a single unifying mission that suffuses the entire culture and galvanizes all aspects of the school. Although curriculum revision is seen as an essential tool in achieving the mission, the emphasis on partnership also extends to such areas as social events, school improvement decisions, hiring, and planning for the future. In the Partnership model, parent involvement is seen not as an addendum, but as an indispensable component of school reform.

There is another difference from the other models. I have suggested that educators are often not fully aware of the model that is guiding their relationships with parents. In contrast, adherents of the Partnership model are actively engaged in defining and constructing a framework for parent involvement and a series of roles for parents that are adpated to the school's mission.

ILLUSTRATIONS

To illustrate the Partnership model, we must draw on comprehensive programs for school reform that include parent involvement as an indispensable element. Characteristic of these programs is that parents are involved in the school in a wide variety of ways and that parents are involved in problem solving and decision making for school improvement.

There are many individual schools where a Partnership model is in effect. I have selected for illustration two variations, the Comer process and the Accelerated Schools program. Both programs have been extensively replicated (at this time, the Comer Process is being implemented in 150 schools in sites all over the country, including California, Virginia, Arkansas, and Kansas; the Accelerated Schools program has been initiated in over 150 schools in 17 states (The role of the National Center, 1992). Both programs have been presented in the professional literature, and I have had an opportunity to study some of these schools directly. Both programs exemplify the wisdom in this quote: "School success is as much an act of social construction undertaken by families and schools as school failure has been shown to be" (McLaughlin & Shields, 1987, p. 158).

The Comer Process or School Development Model

The Comer process (briefly described in Chapter 1; also see Comer, 1980, 1988a, 1988b, 1988c) is an act of social construction whose essence is "the creation of a sense of community and direction for parents, school staff, and students alike" (Comer, quoted in Schorr, 1988, p. 234). Schorr further explains:

Dr. Comer believes that most current attempts at school reform are not sufficiently comprehensive. "People aren't educated in pieces, and kids don't learn in pieces," he says. "That's why it's essential to address the entire social system of the school because of the way the many variables interact and because attitudes, morale, and hope all affect school performance." (p. 235)

The fact sheet about the Comer process circulated by the superintendent of schools in Prince George's County emphasizes the importance of all adults working together to improve the schools. It says:

The key to the Comer process is that schools must make adjustments to bring all adults in the community together in a supportive way—to create an ethos, tone, feeling—that is supportive of children. . . . An additional key aspect of the Comer process is the inclusion of parents in all levels of school activities: SPMT, volunteers, conferencing, "make and takes," PTA, PTO, special programs, sub-committees, etc. Parents are truly welcomed and home-school relationships are fostered. (Murphy, 1987, p. 1)

Comer's philosophy of school improvement makes parent involvement in schools indispensable. He believes that the goal of school reform is to improve the quality of relationships among children and teachers and parents and educators. In his view, learning is not a mechanistic process but a relational one, and emotional attachment and bonding, imitation, identification, and internalization of the attitudes and values of adults are necessary for children to succeed academically (Comer, 1988b). Children will be able to learn only when teachers and parents become allies in a common mission and teachers are able to respond comprehensively to the "whole" child.

In an effort to make this philosophy come alive, I will describe in more detail three of the ways in which parents are involved in Comer schools: as members of the School Planning and Management Team (SPMT), as contributors to curriculum development, and as participants in social and academic activities. My comments are based on a review of the literature about the model and a visit to three Comer schools in Prince George's County, Maryland.

The Comer process is in use in 16 schools in Prince George's County. These 16 schools do not meet desegregation guidelines (90% or more of the children are African-American) and are thus eligible for district funds to support additional staffing and instructional resources. Some of the funds are used to support training in the Comer model for teachers and administrators. In addition, each school is able to hire additional support staff, extend the school day, offer enrichment programs (including transportation), and provide a full computer lab (including some computers that can be taken home).

At the William Beanes School, I attended an SPMT meeting. The SPMT is the centerpiece of the effort to include parents fully in all aspects of school improvement and is a required structural element in any Comer school. Three parents, three educators, and the principal were meeting that day. Their agenda included a discussion of what the principal should do if a child attacks a teacher. The principal explained that the district policy at the elementary level only specified that the response was to be at the principal's discretion. She was seeking input from the group about what the issues were and what her options might be. A rich discussion ensued, with concerns expressed by parents about a consistent policy and the ramifications of the policy for other children. Teachers wanted the policy to be sensitive to the different motives that might prompt inappropriate behavior and the availability of resources to help children before they became aggressive to others. Another item on the agenda was an evaluation of the school's success in meeting the goals of the school improvement plan. The group developed a plan for organizing and reviewing data related to children's attendance, academic and social climate, staff development, and leadership. The principal asked the group many questions, seeking input about the method of data collection and the process to be followed in assessing the data.

My impression as an observer in the group was that parents were not at all hesitant to participate; their views were specifically sought; they seemed to have considerable influence in shaping decisions that were made; the voices of parents did add new and important perspectives; and the issues being discussed were important to establishing a culture in which school improvement was taken seriously.

Parents are also involved in curriculum development in Comer schools. Comer (1980) provides an example from the two pilot schools in New Haven, where teachers asked parents to identify their academic and social objectives for their children and the experiences and skills they felt would help the children attain those objectives. One of the priorities that emerged in the discussion was learning about citizenship and government. Subsequently, parents worked with educators in the planning and execution of a social studies curriculum that included as one of its components the staging of a debate among the current candidates for mayor of New Haven. Students learned about writing invitations, interviewing politicians, debating major issues, and expressing appreciation to the speakers. Parents were as involved as the students in preparing for the debate, and the audience at the school included large numbers of parents and community members as well as educators and students.

At the Berkshire School, as in many of the schools in Prince George's County, the population is not a stable one. Forty-six percent of the children leave every year. The principal, Dr. Rita Robinson, explained that families were suffering from deteriorating economic conditions and inability to keep up with housing costs. Consequently, this principal focused on creating enjoyable social events that would welcome new and returning parents and support the development of informal relationships between parents and school personnel. Two hundred mothers had come to the mothers' breakfast the day before, straining the capacity of the cafeteria. An event called "Pot Luck in the Park" drew enormous crowds a month or so earlier and was offered all day on a Saturday, with full teacher participation. An in-service activity for parents on the upcoming science fair introduced parents to the problem-solving orientation of the activity and offered inexpensive materials (construction paper, oak tag backboards to frame the project) so they could "get a head start." Dr. Robinson explained that she encourages parents to come to visit the school any time. She said, "I tell them; I mean it; the leader has to live it."

At this school, the emphasis on valuing relationships and supporting the development of the whole child seemed palpable. Beautiful flowers from a teacher's garden were on a table in the front hall. Photos and names of all the staff were displayed there too, along with a big sign reading "Welcome to Our Guests." Photo albums on a table near the office recorded important school and home events, and another wall was devoted to "Feature Family of the Month." Children's successes were applauded everywhere: Posters documented perfect attendance; reading buttons with students' names on them were displayed for the many prolific readers. Birthdays were recognized and celebrated in the library every Friday, and "Fantastic Friday" provided an opportunity for a rotating group of children to engage in blowing bubbles or other activities "just for fun."

Although not part of our itinerary, teachers surprised the principal and our small visiting group by preparing a homemade lunch. Teachers seemed genuinely eager to welcome visitors to the classroom so they could demonstrate what they were doing and how proud they were of "their" children. Despite the extreme poverty in the neighborhood and the turnover of children, children's scores on the California Achievement Test were at the national average.

The flagship of these 16 Comer schools, the Columbia Park School, has received extensive national recognition because of the achievement of its students "against the odds." Children's scores in math on the California Achievement Test were at the 96th percentile level in 1990, and average reading achievement scores were above the 50th percentile.

Many plaques, awards, a Presidential flag, and framed newspaper articles celebrating the children's achievements decorated the walls, and children's science projects were on view in the hallways.

In each of the three schools I visited, the involvement of parents was comprehensive and was intricately connected to the mission of school improvement.

The Accelerated Schools Model

Levin (1987, 1988a, 1988b; Hopfenberg et al., 1990) has initiated an experimental program called Accelerated Schools, that offers another comprehensive approach to school reform and parent involvement. Launched in 1986 in two schools in low-income communities in and near San Francisco, the program has as its mission to accelerate the learning of children at risk so that they perform at grade level by the end of the sixth grade.

The three cornerstones of educational reform according to the Accelerated Schools model include

1. An interdisciplinary *accelerated curriculum* emphasizing first-hand experience, language-rich classrooms, problem solving, and higher order analytical skills.
2. *Instructional practices* that promote active learning experiences, draw on peer tutoring and cooperative learning strategies, and focus on the teacher as a facilitator and communicator of information.
3. An *organizational model* that is characterized by the broad participation of administrators, teachers, and parents. (The principal facilitates collaborative decision making and flexible scheduling, and faculty committees are the locus for developing and evaluating experimental approaches to school improvement in priority areas of the mission, as explained more fully in Hopfenberg et al., 1990.)

The Accelerated model rejects a technocratic approach to schooling (where a teacher-technician communicates knowledge to a student-subject), any remedial strategy that is focused on mechanics and repetition for teaching children at risk, and a bureaucratic approach to school organization that relies on mandates and regulations from above.

The school culture the Accelerated model seeks to create is one whose principles include unity of purpose (a common mission defining common goals among adults and students); empowerment coupled with responsibility (key participants can make the important decisions at the school); and building on strengths of all participants. The values the model strives to embody include equity for all students, participation, open communication, reflection, experimentation, trust, and risk-taking.

I visited the Hoover School in Redwood City, California, a community that is low income and 95% Latino. I was very impressed with the high energy, commitment, excitement, and hard work that were evident among students, teachers, administrators, and parents. The school was in its second year of implementing the model, and a transformation in parent involvement had already occurred. For example, parents were very active on the school's steering committee (8 parents, 8 teachers or support personnel, and the principal). When I asked a parent about her role on the steering committee, she said that the principal had insisted that the parents have a say. Contributions of parents were also tangible: When this parent said crossing guards were needed, they were hired.

Parents were active as volunteers and paid aides. A parent aide explained to me that she liked her work very much because she was assigned to the kindergarten every day and was involved in teaching children, not just "using machines." Parents were eager to support the school. The night before I visited, for example, over 80 families had gotten together to raise funds to improve school security. Parents made and sold handicrafts and food, and $300 was raised within an hour in this low-income community.

Parents were involved in their children's learning. Almost every family had pledged to attend conferences and Back-to-School night and to spend 15 minutes of quality time with each child daily. A program in Family Math (a 6-week program for children, parents, and teachers that foouoes on learning math concepts through enjoyable activities that can be extended at home) needed to be offered twice to meet demand. The school had initiated an extended day program and a counseling program in the evenings for children at risk.

Despite the high levels of parent involvement, expanding involvement was one of the three major priorities of the school for the year. A faculty committee used a problem-solving, "inquiry" method to analyze which parents were still not involved and what the committee could do to change that pattern. The principal explained to me that his most important future goal was to have "full-blown parent involvement," where involvement could be seen in a multitude of ways inside and outside the school. He wanted every parent to feel that he or she could fit in, no matter what, and he was most eager to connect with parents of low-achieving children.

There was no question that parent involvement had been transformed in the 2 years that the program had been in operation. Equally striking was the fact that scores on national skills tests, though not yet at the national average, had increased 10 percentile points in one year.

More recent data are available from Hoover's sister school in California, Daniel Webster. The Summer 1991 newsletter *Accelerated Schools* documented that at the end of the fourth year of implementation of the Accelerated Schools model, the Webster children had made significant achievement gains. Although other schools in the district showed slight declines, Webster students showed an average increase in math scores on the California Test of Basic Skills of 19 percentile points, with all grades performing above grade level. Some grades gained as much as 20 percentile points in language, and most classes improved over 10 percentile points in reading and language. However, though improving dramatically, the reading and language scores had not yet reached the national average.

EVALUATION

A true partnership is a transforming vision of school culture based on collegiality, experimentation for school improvement, mutual support, and joint problem solving. It is based on the assumption that parents and educators are members of a partnership who have a common goal: generally, improving the school or supporting the success of all children in school. Although parents and educators may have different contributions to make to the partnership and educators may be primarily responsible for initiating it, the assumption is that the common mission cannot be accomplished without collaboration.

Educators and parents who have adopted the Comer process or the Accelerated Schools program are committed to creating a school culture in which all children can be successful. Both programs include parents, community members, educators, and children in learning partnerships; they create enriched curricula and cultures; they evaluate their practices and results; and they use collaborative problem solving to address issues that emerge through evaluation. Such schools are most likely to have children achieving at grade level, even with high concentrations of children at risk. The emphasis on equity, shared power, accountability, and experimentation seems to sustain energy and ownership among the partners.

The Accelerated Schools program places more emphasis on curriculum than does the Comer process; curricular and instructional practices are not an explicit focus in the Comer schools. The Comer process places more emphasis on a developmentally based, coordinated program of support services for children and adults. The Student Staff Support Team is a structure developed by Comer that has no analogue in Levin's model.

The disadvantage of the Partnership model is that it is hard to implement. Both the Comer and Accelerated Schools programs demand a commitment to continual reflection, inquiry, and evaluation in the context of jobs with multiple moment-to-moment responsibilities. Both require exchanging the traditional isolation of the educator's role for a collaborative role, and the development of new patterns of scheduling and interaction to support this role. Both require a leader who is also a facilitator and a cheerleader, as well as school and district policies that support the effort. These requirements will be discussed more fully in Chapters 9 and 10.

FOUR ELEMENTS OF A TRUE PARTNERSHIP BETWEEN HOME AND SCHOOL

The most commonly used typology for parent involvement is Joyce Epstein's, which has provided a very useful starting point for schools eager to expand their outreach to families. For reference, the Epstein (1987) typology for parent involvement includes

1. Basic obligations of families, including health, safety, and a positive home environment
2. Basic obligations of schools, including conferences with parents regarding their child's programs and progress
3. Parent involvement at school, including volunteer activities and support for sports and student performances
4. Parent involvement in learning activities at home, including supervising homework and helping children work on skills that will help them learn in the classroom
5. Parent involvement in governance, decision making, and advocacy, including participation in parent–teacher organizations and in various decision-making and advisory roles.

Building on Epstein's useful typology, I have developed a framework that outlines the most important elements of a partnership between home and school. It differs from Epstein's model in stressing the mutuality of interaction between home and school and condensing the list to four elements, as follows:

1. *Creating two-way communication.* Parents and educators both have vital information to share. Educators share information with parents about children's progress in school; their expectations and hopes for

the school and the children; and their curriculum, policies, and programs. Parents share information with educators about their child's needs, strengths, and background; and their expectations and hopes for the school and their child. Educators and parents listen to each other. Ideally, the result is parents and educators who are informed, who have created a negotiated set of joint expectations for children and the school, and who work together to create a school environment in which all can learn and feel successful.

2. *Enhancing learning at home and at school.* Parents contribute to children's learning by having high expectations, providing a setting that allows concentrated work, supporting and nurturing learning that occurs in school and elsewhere, and offering love, discipline, guidance, and encouragement. Educators develop curriculum and instructional practices and strong relationships with children that create conditions for optimal learning. Parents and educators develop an array of ways in which parents can be involved in and out of the classroom to enrich children's learning. Parents understand what is occurring in the curriculum and ways in which they can monitor, assist, or extend children's homework. Parents might function in the school as paid aides or volunteers, participants in educational activities offered at school for the family, or contributors to curriculum selection and enrichment.

3. *Providing mutual support.* Educators support parents by offering educational programs for them that are responsive to their interests and needs. Parents support educators in many ways, such as volunteering in schools, organizing and planning activities, raising money, and attending functions (plays, sports events). Educators and parents build trusting relationships and arrange occasions to acknowledge and celebrate each other's contributions to children's growth. Increasingly, the school becomes the critical institution in the community for linking parents with useful health, education, and social services.

4. *Making joint decisions.* Parents and educators work together to improve the school through participation on councils, committees, and planning and management teams. Parents and educators are involved in joint problem solving at every level: individual child, classroom, school, and district.

SUMMARY

The Partnership model offers a new vision for schools, in which the culture is transformed to encompass strong relationships among parents, educators, and community personnel. A spirit of experimentation and inquiry infuses the learning of children and adults, and the school becomes a community that cultivates the strengths and supports the success of all its members. In the Partnership model, parents and educators work collaboratively to achieve a common mission (generally, success for all children). Parents and other important family members are seen as vital to the success of the mission.

The Comer process and Accelerated Schools programs were presented as examples of the Partnership model, and the advantages and disadvantages of the Partnership model were briefly sketched.

Finally, four elements of a true partnership were outlined: creating two-way communication, enhancing learning at home and at school, providing mutual support, and making joint decisions. Suggestions for how to develop these elements will be the subject of the remainder of the book.

CHAPTER 5

Establishing Two-Way Communication

This chapter begins the "how to" section of this book, where specific guidelines and suggestions are offered for implementing home–school partnerships, and each of the elements of partnership outlined in the previous chapter is explored in turn. One does not need to be fully committed to a Partnership model to read further. The approach to parent involvement that is selected in a school needs to reflect community priorities, traditions, and hopes for the future. Although the model of full partnership provides the frame for weaving together all the suggestions that follow, there are many ideas here that could be utilized regardless of philosophy.

Nonetheless, there are two reasons to consider committing to the challenge of fully implementing a Partnership model. The first reason is practical: The Partnership model has the best track record for contributing to significant school improvement in schools where there are important discontinuities between home and school and where large numbers of children are not succeeding.

The second reason is based on the need to be explicit about the values we support and teach through our schools. There is mounting concern that even in schools where youngsters are doing well academically, their ability to work with others from diverse backgrounds, their willingness to accept responsibility for their actions, and their motivation to contribute to the larger community are decreasing (Ribadeneira, 1990). The implementation of the full Partnership model prefigures in schools the kind of society that America could become in the twenty-first century: a society based on democratic exchange, equity, pluralistic membership, trusting relationships, high expectations and ideals, collaborative problem solving, reflection, and continuous learning. For our children to succeed in the struggle that they will face to develop solutions to the challenges of the next century, they will need vision, collaborative skills, and clearly defined values as well as academic competence. If students could be educated in a school that is based on the principles of partnership, they might have a head start in developing the skills that will enable them to be future leaders.

Some key terms need to be clarified as we explore how to initiate home–school collaboration. The "parents" in parent involvement are defined broadly, encompassing not just biological parents, but step-parents, grandparents, primary caretakers, older siblings, aunts, and uncles. Because family structures are so varied, it is important to welcome all family members or primary caretakers *who have special responsibilities for or special meaning to the child.* The hope is that school personnel will communicate with at least one family member of each child in the school, and that parent involvement activities will attract not just parent activists, but families who are traditionally underrepresented.

Generally we talk about parent involvement in schools, but in this book the locus of involvement is broader, encompassing homes and neighborhood or community settings, such as churches, community agencies, youth centers, or athletic facilities. A broader definition is useful because there are times when parents are uneasy about, unwilling, or unable to come to school, but are still interested in talking with educators about their children. It is often possible to begin dialogues in such circumstances on more neutral territory. There are also times when children and parents are best served through coordination of the services of more than one institution in the community. School personnel and parents may be participants in such activities without necessarily having them located in the school.

The final important clarification is that parent involvement is not seen as an end in itself, but as a means to the "end" or goal of parents and educators working together to enhance the academic and social growth of children (see Davies, 1990a). Given this goal, both parents and educators have a responsibility to improve the conditions of schooling so that success for all children can be sought. Accomplishing this goal is very challenging for parents and educators, because it demands that parents invest more fully in the school and in all the school's children, and that educators share authority with parents.

THE GOALS OF TWO-WAY COMMUNICATION

Learning how to communicate effectively is essential for developing a partnership between home and school. This chapter will describe how to build the scaffolding that supports a rich exchange between parents and educators. Each contribution (e.g., developing a parent involvement policy, creating informal opportunities for communication, making parents feel welcome at school, clarifying mutual expectations) builds a stronger network of mutual support.

There are three key indicators that effective two-way communication is being established.

1. More families are involved.
2. Families are involved in a wider variety of ways over a significant period of time.
3. The involvement is experienced on both sides as constructive and purposeful.

But there is no single formula for reaching out: Each school should decide on the pattern of activities and structures that is especially suited to its mission and local circumstances.

There is also no need to implement all the ideas suggested in this chapter. Although the broad categories are useful reference points, selecting only certain activities from the array provided or developing altogether different activities that are more suitable for one's own site is most appropriate. In fact, the collaborative process of making these decisions may be as important as the programs or activities that are launched.

To return to our analogy, the construction of a sturdy scaffolding requires thoughtful selection of materials, careful workmanship, and time. Ideally, the suggestions in this chapter will prepare school personnel and parents to initiate discussions, make choices, adapt suggestions, and set a realistic timetable for implementation.

CREATING A CULTURE THAT SUPPORTS
TWO-WAY COMMUNICATION

The District's Role

Although neither a necessary nor sufficient condition for good home–school communication, a district policy that supports parent involvement is very useful. The San Diego City Schools District is the first large urban district in the nation to have a comprehensive, board-approved policy for parent involvement. The policy states:

> The Board of Education recognizes the necessity and value of parent involvement to support student success and academic achievement. In order

to assure collaborative partnerships between parents and schools, the board, working through the administration, is committed to:

a. involving parents as partners in school governance including shared decision making and advisory functions.

b. establishing effective two-way communication with all parents, respecting the diversity and differing needs of families.

c. developing strategies and programmatic structures at schools to enable parents to participate actively in their children's education.

d. providing support and coordination for school staff and parents to implement and sustain appropriate parent involvement from kindergarten through grade twelve.

e. utilizing schools to connect students and families with community resources that provide educational enrichment and support. (Chrispeels, Fernandez, & Preston, 1990, p. 3)

Both the policy and the implementation strategies initiated by the San Diego City Schools deserve careful attention. At the instigation of the superintendent of schools, the Parent Involvement Programs Department of the Community Relations and Integration Services Division in San Diego selected a very powerful task force of almost 50 parents, teachers, administrators, and community representatives to function as a work group. In a series of spirited meetings with much debate, the task force hammered out the policy that was subsequently approved by the Board of Education and distributed as part of a handbook for principals.

The task force also developed a 3-year implementation plan, characterized as a centrally supported, bottom-up approach to implementation. It included three components.

1. *Building Staff Capacity.* To achieve this, workshops on parent involvement were provided to principals, parents, and staff; incentive grants to support parent involvement activities were offered on a competitive basis to 16 schools throughout the district; and research information and materials for parent involvement were collected, summarized, and widely distributed.

2. *Partnership Development.* To plan and implement comprehensive parent involvement programs in schools, the Community Relations Division provided principals with a planning process for improving parent involvement and a format for evaluating current practices. A major conference on parent involvement was held for 700 participants in the first year of the program, and community-based organizations as well as other divisions in the district have also been providing leadership and training on parent involvement in schools.

3. *Follow-up and Support.* In the following 2 years, the staff of this division worked to clarify procedures; provided assistance to schools as requested on needs assessment, staff training, implementation, volunteer programs, and evaluation; provided financial support for innovative programs; coordinated district and community resources; and implemented an evaluation plan.

This policy has sparked much parent involvement in the San Diego City Schools. The money, administrative support, and training provided at the district level have encouraged innovative programs. The involvement of a large network of powerful people in the community and in the schools has built consensus about the importance of parent involvement and generated a comprehensive network of linked resources to support and help implement it. Moreover, each principal is now expected to develop a plan for developing home–school partnership in his or her school (see Chrispeels, 1991).

Districts can also support parent involvement in schools by not issuing other policies that directly or indirectly undermine parent involvement efforts. Zeldin (1990) makes this point, explaining that if districts develop good policies but then fail to fund them for a significant period of time, fail to provide paid time for any joint activities, or create decision-making structures that do not bring parents and educators together, the policies are not likely to stimulate lasting change.

The School's Role

Parent outreach is ultimately carried out by teachers and principals at the building level. Zeldin (1990) explains:

> State and district mandates can facilitate or diminish the change process, but ultimately, it is the school staff—the policy implementors—who make the initiative work. If building administrators and teachers do not perceive a need for change, or have the necessary tools to make changes, neither pressure nor support from state and district will result in successful implementation. (p. 29)

Principals. Principals can build a climate that supports parent involvement in several ways: by creating a school policy that supports parent involvement, by hiring teachers who enjoy working with parents, by evaluating personnel on their success in working with families, and by modeling successful outreach to parents. Principals can also share research findings, support in-service training, and initiate an evaluation of existing practices. Another key contribution of the principal would be to experiment with scheduling to make sure that time and space are generously allocated to support parent–educator communication. The principal can also encourage teachers to move in this direction by building group investment and excitement about the challenge and rewards of parent involvement, offering educational opportunities for group members, and celebrating and consolidating gains (see Swap, 1990c).

The available research supports the importance of the principal's role in creating a culture that supports outreach to parents. For example, in a study of second-grade classrooms in several schools, Hauser-Cram (1983) discovered that there was significantly more parent involvement when principals established an explicit policy encouraging such involvement. Epstein (1987) discovered that administrative policies in different school systems seemed to promote the use of certain types of parent involvement, and that administrative leadership was related to levels of parent involvement in different schools.

Teachers. Teachers are the key agents for reaching out to parents. Whether they choose to do so depends on several factors. Epstein and Dauber (1991) report that teachers who perceived high support for parent involvement from their colleagues and from parents had more positive attitudes toward parent involvement. Moreover, teachers were more apt to make frequent and diverse contacts with parents if they taught self-contained classes with limited numbers of students. The authors also reported that "the attitudes and practices of the teachers, not the education, socioeconomic status, or marital status of the parent, were the important variables for understanding whether parents were knowledgeable and successful partners with the schools in their children's education" (pp. 1–2).

Another important factor in teachers' willingness to reach out to parents may be whether they feel supported and empowered in school themselves. Teachers are unlikely to share with parents the responsibility for educating children unless they feel they are seen as responsible by principals; they are unlikely to share decisions with parents unless they feel that they have the authority to share in decision making as well. Thus, the school culture that would be most favorable to reaching out to parents is one in which the staff felt strong and secure, empowered to make important decisions about their work life, and eager for more information and resources that would help them to fully educate children.

Teachers often feel that parent outreach is an added burden. Many do not expect that parents will be particularly responsive to their efforts and are not convinced that they have the knowledge and skills to work with parents. Therefore, the transition to new behaviors and attitudes is complex (see Krasnow, 1990b). Several strategies help to make this transition easier: exposure to evidence that parent involvement is effective and rewarding for teachers, the opportunity to visit good programs, training in parent involvement strategies, opportunities to shape the pace and design of programs, and support and appreciation for their initiatives.

Parents. The third group that must contribute to creating a culture where parent involvement is seen as essential to educating children is, of course, the parents. Though some parents are committed to being involved in school and find it easy to interact with school personnel to support this joint mission, most do not. The remainder of the chapter will explore ways of developing positive relationships with parents, discovering how families might contribute to their children's success in and out of school, and learning how parents and educators can share information, hopes, and expectations about children and learning.

BUILDING THE SCAFFOLDING

Creating Informal Opportunities for Communication

One of the most important ways to initiate positive relationships with family members is to plan informal social gatherings that include both food and opportunities for informal conversation. These gatherings might occur in school or at a familiar community gathering spot such as library, agency, or park. As I concluded at the end of a 2-year research study of urban schools reaching out to parents:

> It seems clear that when there has not been a history of parent involvement in a school (or involvement among all subgroups or parents), school or classroom-based activities that promote pleasant social encounters and exchange of information among adults are indispensable. These activities, usually supplemented by food and informal conversation, provide a mechanism for parents and teachers to develop an acquaintance as "just people," creating a context for an array of additional activities or joint projects. It seems that these types of activities signal a mutual interest in establishing adult relationships on behalf of the child and in breaking down the barriers between home and school that seem inevitable in urban communities. Social events continue to be needed over time, to draw in new parents and educators and to help all the adult members of the community to appreciate the rituals that are valued among the adults. (Swap, 1990c, p. 110)

The director of the national Schools Reaching Out (SRO) Project also came to appreciate the value of "events and activities that emphasized socializing, fun, good food, all the light hearted fare" as a "sign of caring," and a step toward developing good relationships and a climate of trust (Davies, 1990b, p. 42). He further explains:

> My own reaction to the emphasis on "light fare" was somewhat skeptical. I have written and given speeches decrying the trivializing of parent involvement and have engaged in my share of bake-sale bashing.
>
> Our SRO experience convinces me that I was wrong. If the partnership and reaching out efforts never move past muffins, the primary objective of success for all children won't be well-served. But these seemingly trivial little things should be seen as essential lubrication for more serious interventions. (p. 42)

Vivian Johnson (1990; personal communication, October 22, 1990) has helped me to understand *why* these informal social events are necessary and important, and why seemingly unimportant aspects of the occasion, such as the quality of the food, the ethnic appropriateness of the food, even the smells of good cooking, can signal (perhaps more profoundly than what educators say) a welcoming attitude toward parents. Concern about these details conveys an effort to welcome parents as equals, as we do guests in our own home.

Illustrations. Some of the types of informal events that seem to have prompted good attendance even in schools with no tradition of parent involvement have included

- *Welcome-Back-to-School events* for families to meet new and continuing staff. Examples include a multicultural potluck dinner with a short program of readings from different languages and ethnic dancing; an "Allcomers-Newcomers Picnic" on a Saturday; a "Potluck in the Park" event with competitions and fun activities such as a water slide. In addition, activities for parents whose children are attending the school for the first time are worth doing, such as a welcoming coffee before school starts for parents of newly entering kindergarten or middle school children.
- *Family member breakfasts.* These are also good get-acquainted activities; typically, mothers, fathers, grandparents, or other significant family members are invited to school to share breakfast and talk informally with teachers about the curriculum, goals for the year, or other topics.

- *Holiday events or other celebrations.* Potluck Thanksgiving celebrations (sometimes organized by individual classroom teachers), celebrations of Three Kings Day, bilingual fairs, and spaghetti dinners are only a few examples of events that can bring families into the school in a festive mood. Because parents and other family members are very likely to come to children's performances, school personnel might wish to combine a performance with an informal reception for families.

Suggestions for Making Events Successful. Even though these events seem informal and comfortable, careful planning is needed to ensure that invited families actually attend activities and leave feeling that their time was well spent.

- *Strategies for reaching parents.* Suggestions include providing advance notice (at least 2 weeks and preferably a month); preparing personal invitations (from teachers, another parent, a child, or child and teacher); scheduling at least some events on weekends or before or after school hours to accommodate working schedules; setting up a telephone chain; inviting returning parents to bring a parent who is new to the school; sending reminders home; and even holding competitions (with a desirable prize) to see which class can boast highest attendance by family members.
- *Strategies for making attendance easier.* Transportation and child care are the familiar needs of parents. Some schools arrange car pools or transport parents in school buses. High school students in child development classes may be recruited to babysit, or activities for children can be part of the event itself. Not having to plan a meal at home in addition to arranging to attend an event can be an incentive to come, especially if families know the food will be good!
- *Planning events carefully to promote informal communication.* Ironic as this may sound, sometimes informal events that are planned to promote home–school communication take place without parents and educators actually talking to each other. For example, parents and teachers may sit at separate tables during a potluck dinner, or a teacher may be monopolized for the duration of the event by one parent with a serious concern. Thinking about "mixed" seating arrangements, fun activities that would pair teachers and parents, and programs that include contributions by parents and educators are some of the ways around this natural tendency we all have to stay with people we already know. Planning how food will be arranged and how to make "traffic" flow smoothly can also support good communication.

- *Evaluating activities.* In the beginning stages of attracting parents to school, educators tend to be very disappointed if fewer people come than were expected. Instead, educators should focus on warmly welcoming and valuing the parents who *do* come and comforting event planners with the idea that it is great that *this* group of parents gave up time in their busy schedule to attend. Word of mouth is one of the best strategies for recruiting additional people, and if those who do come share their good experiences, then more family members are likely to come in the future. Another useful strategy in planning for future events is asking parents for a formal or informal evaluation of activities so that the planning of subsequent events is influenced by their feedback.

Creating a Welcoming Atmosphere in School

The physical appearance of the building and the few encounters a parent has on the way to his or her destination in school can encourage or discourage involvement. It is not unusual, especially in an inner city location, for a parent to find an imposing building surrounded by a chain link fence, an entrance door that is locked and where long delays follow the ringing of the bell, a gruff security guard or a series of maze-like corridors that need to be negotiated without direction, and an office secretary who assiduously avoids making eye contact.

Schools that create a welcoming atmosphere look and feel very different—right away. The key is avoiding a foreboding, institutional atmosphere and creating a more home-like, human-scale environment. A clean and brightly lit building is essential. In addition, schools can

- Display signs that welcome visitors (If English is a second language for many parents, add welcome signs that reflect the language of families' countries of origin.)
- Post a map that explains where the office is
- Arrange flowers, brightly colored murals, children's pictures, other displays, and/or photographs in an entrance hallway
- Designate space for a parent center and have coffee, tea, or cold drinks available
- Assign a parent to greet other parents at the entrance of the school at drop-off and pick-up times during the first week of school
- Explain to secretaries their importance in supporting family involvement and brainstorm a variety of strategies for welcoming and supporting parents
- Arrange for translators for parents who do not speak English.

Teachers and administrators can also be individually welcoming. Many principals have "visiting hours" as well as visits by appointment, and many teachers write welcoming letters home to parents within the first few weeks of school. Newsletters composed by teachers or principals can be welcoming, appreciative, and informative for parents. Some teachers telephone families at the beginning of the year to chat informally and to invite further communication by appointment or at designated call-in times that are most convenient for them. Technology has made connecting with parents easier for some schools: For example, teachers have prepared videos for parents that portray their children in action. Even if parents have difficulty coming in during school hours, they can borrow the tape and feel somewhat informed about their child's experiences in school.

Parent centers in schools can be a focal point for organizing more home–school communication and parent involvement in school. A parent center demonstrates that parents are important enough to the school to deserve a room of their own. At the Ellis School in Roxbury, Massachusetts, the two part-time coordinators of the parent center provided educational information to parents, advised parents in person and over the telephone about obtaining food and housing, greeted parents arriving at school with their children, solicited and deployed parent volunteers in classrooms, communicated with parents in Spanish, and offered the space for parent meetings and classes (Krasnow, 1990b).

Teachers also found the center a welcoming place, and came by during free moments to use the telephone, browse through literature, have a cup of coffee, and chat with parents. Reporting on her observations and interviews at this center, Johnson (1990) concluded that the "Parent Center is a helping place and that the 'good news' is spreading through the neighborhood. . . . The Parent Center serves as a place where strengths and resources of parents and community are shared with the school for mutual benefit" (p. 23).

School personnel can also be welcoming to families outside of the context of the school building. For example, *parent outreach programs* (where trained parents pay visits to other parents' homes) can be very effective in making contact with parents who do not ordinarily come to school. Outreach workers can share information between home and school, exchange hints on home learning activities or child-rearing strategies, advocate for families in need to the school or other agencies, and support parents as they learn how to work the system themselves. Often these visits establish a personal bond and therefore make it easier for parents to participate in activities at school. (For more detailed descriptions, see Johnson, 1990, or Cochran, 1987.) In some systems, the teachers have become the outreach workers. In Rochester, New York, for example, teachers are doing home visiting as an essential component of their jobs, and their salaries have been boosted to compensate them for their extra time.

CLARIFYING THE SCHOOL'S HOPES AND EXPECTATIONS

As we saw in Chapter 1, parent involvement is increased if parents feel that their involvement is important and valued by school personnel. Obvious as it sounds, one way to convey this message is to say so—at open houses, at parent meetings, in newsletters, in policy statements. One principal announced his arrival at a school by inviting all the parents to the school to meet him. He talked about his expectations for the children, the school, and parent involvement and asked parents to share their hopes and concerns. The meeting was very well attended, and parents expressed afterward that they felt that this principal really wanted to hear from them. It does not take long for this message to be believed if it is repeatedly stated and specific opportunities for involvement are explained and supported.

It is easy for both parents and educators to be confused about what to expect from each other. Expectations are established by tradition and culture. I have already outlined four quite different models of involvement, each of which is in use in some settings. In addition to these contrasting models that have roots in American traditions, parents who have emigrated from other countries bring with them expectations for school involvement based on customs in their own countries. However, even if it is not what they are used to, most parents are willing to become involved if they become convinced that their involvement will contribute to their child's success. The type of involvement required should be within the family's capacity (e.g., parent education workshops offered in English may not be attractive to parents with limited proficiency in English) and not incongruent with important family values. In the spirit of two-way communication, it is useful if that involvement can be mutually negotiated.

Contracts

Several schools have demonstrated their commitment to parent involvement by preparing home–school contracts and seeking one hundred percent endorsement from families. A strategy most often adopted in urban environments, the contract seeks to secure parental agreement to do such things as participate in school events (e.g., conferences, open house night); support the child's academic growth at home (e.g., providing a quiet place to study, reviewing homework, reading to the child); and prepare the child for school (e.g., making sure the child gets to school on time and has eaten breakfast).

Ideally, the contract would also specify what school personnel agreed to do and would be co-signed by the child's teacher, principal, or both. For example, school personnel could agree to provide timely information about each child's progress; to respond to any parental concerns or questions within 2 days; to provide information to parents about how to support short- and long-term homework assignments; and to provide access to resources that would extend children's learning (e.g., summer reading lists, tutorial programs, enrichment activities).

The contract should not reflect a deficit model in its approach to parents or educators. Ideally, a task force of parents and educators could create an initial draft of the contract to avoid inappropriate content or tone.

Open House Activities

Inviting parents to the school to see the classrooms and speak to teachers and administrators can be a good way to communicate information and expectations. It is useful for parents to be able to associate real people with the names they have seen and to be able to visualize the spaces that their children inhabit every day. On these occasions, teachers often share information about their curriculum and methods, and clarify their expectations for children and parents.

Schools might consider any of several formats, such as open house week (where parents are invited to visit the classroom in operation any time during a designated week), grade level open houses, or monthly open houses. Any of these strategies that invite repeated contact or contact within smaller groups tend to create more opportunity for genuine interchange. Inviting parents to the school before the school year begins (with or without children) takes advantage of everyone's optimism about the new year and sends a message of interest in collaboration "right from the start."

Some schools have experimented with activities for parents that allow them to experience firsthand some of the children's daily enterprises. A kindergarten teacher, for example, allowed parents to choose among activities at several learning stations and then asked parents to brainstorm what cognitive, social, or motor skills might be supported by children's work with, for example, puzzles or the water table. Another teacher showed slides of the children in action over a typical day to convey a sense of the daily schedule and her goals. Parents of older children might be asked to review their children's texts and work folders as well as to try out some typical assignments.

This general information is often very useful to parents. As a parent, I have also found that specific information from teachers about future events, homework schedules, and expectations for the class is a useful supplement.

In the spirit of two-way communication, these occasions could also be used to discover what parents hope their children might learn; to identify resources that parents might be able to share; to invite comments about curriculum, pedagogy, or goals; and to make it very clear what opportunities parents might have to continue a dialogue with school personnel about individual children or school issues. (See "Hearing from Parents," next section, for additional ideas.)

Newsletters and Notes Home

Establishing a channel for regular communication is one of the best ways to underline what is important at the school over time. A principal's monthly newsletter can identify goals, celebrate successes, announce meetings, offer tips for home-learning activities, and make announcements. To encourage two-way communication, articles, letters, and questions from parents could be solicited.

One principal in a large urban elementary school, for example, had established a school-wide goal of increasing children's language skills. Over the course of a year, his monthly newsletters provided a record of the many activities at home and in school that took place to support this goal. For example, parents were asked to read aloud to their children on a daily basis (parents who did were recognized in an "Honor Roll" that was reported in the newsletter). The newsletter announced activities that supported this effort (e.g., workshops for parents on "Reading Aloud to Your Children"; "The Writing Process"; "Beginning Reading"; "Helping Your Child With Homework"). The principal addressed a meeting of the Parents Association to explain the language arts program and suggest how parents could be involved. (A report of this event was included in the newsletter.) The newsletter contained information about increases in children's reading scores and announced a luncheon for parents and teachers to celebrate this achievement. Book lists and tips for language arts activities that could be done at home were regularly included.

Data suggested that these several activities made parents very much aware of the school's goal for their children and how they could help achieve it. In a questionnaire sent to parents at the end of the year, most parents volunteered the information that the school was helping their children in reading and reported that they tried to read to their child every day.

Teachers can also use newsletters or notes home to announce goals and expectations, report on progress, celebrate successes, ask for help, or give information to parents about individual children. Some teachers exchange notebooks with parents on a daily or weekly basis. (Both write comments in the notebooks that help them to monitor the youngster's progress and their responses to it.)

Policy Handbooks

Some schools offer parents a handbook that presents school policies on such subjects as attendance, grading, health issues, early childhood screening, discipline codes and procedures, homework, special assistance for children, release days, and other useful topics. Telephone numbers of key people and calendars are often included. Some schools also develop handbooks on specific topics such as special education policies or summer opportunities for children. It is useful for a team of parents and educators to work on these handbooks together and to have them translated into languages that are commonly used in the community.

HEARING FROM PARENTS

In addition to listening to parents during meetings, a policy of two-way communication would ensure that parents have comprehensive and on-going opportunities to contribute information, share expectations, and augment the resources of the school. Here are some examples.

Information Forms

Parents could fill out a child information form for the teacher at the beginning of the year, alerting the teacher to their child's special interests and strengths, the parents' learning goals for the child, any concerns or issues, and any other information that the parent (or child) would like the teacher to know (see Appendix A).

Because of the many different kinds of family structures today, it is important that schools' standard requests for family information be sensitively developed. Family members may not have the same last names; custody decisions may compel release of the child to only one of the parents; the child's primary caretaker may not be a parent; family members at different addresses may both wish to receive vital information concerning a child's progress. (See Appendix B for an example of a family information form that was carefully developed by school personnel.)

In the absence of a context of trust, what may seem like very minor details to school personnel during busy registration times can seem like major portents to parents. For example, a mother of biracial twins who was registering them for kindergarten became very upset when a registration form required her to check whether the twins were Caucasian or black. When she expressed her distress, the administrator said, "You have to decide, and if you don't check one, we'll choose for you." This incident and a few others caused this mother to feel that hers was the "wrong kind of family" and that she was not welcome in this school.

Needs Assessments

Another way to establish two-way communication is to ask parents to identify their needs, interests, or attitudes in relation to the school. Such an inquiry, often called a needs assessment, can be conducted by a teacher, a school, a district, or a parent organization. (See Appendix C for examples.) School personnel may be interested in knowing any number of things: for example, how parents might like to contribute to the school; what concerns they have about their children's education; what hopes they might have for future programs, activities, or services; what educational programs they might be interested in. (A recent survey in my town, responding to a crisis in school revenues, sought parents' advice about their priorities for reductions in programs, personnel, and supplies!) In my experience, even small-scale efforts to collect information can be very productive, and parents are usually very pleased when the school takes an interest in their opinions *and* uses this information for planning programs. On the other hand, ambitious efforts that require extensive resources to analyze may lead to volunteer burnout, and questionnaires that seem to promise responsiveness to all parent requests may cause misunderstanding.

In addition to written questionnaires, school personnel (or parent groups) can gain information about parents' perspectives through individual interviews, structured group interactions, or a combination of written and interpersonal formats. (For a more complete discussion of how to conduct a needs assessment, design instruments, conduct individual and group interviews, and use the information collected, see Swap, 1987.)

Developing a School Mission

Parents could be invited to participate in a general discussion to consider the mission and priorities of the school. Generally the reason for writing a mission statement is to develop widespread consensus and community support for a comprehensive effort to improve the school. "Key people are encouraged to envision the future and develop strategies to achieve that future" (Thornton, 1990, p. 2).

The process of developing a vision and carrying it out needs to be carefully managed. One useful resource is a manual and accompanying videotapes that are available from the California Department of Education. These documents provide a detailed description of a sequential, data-based process to accomplish school reform that has been used to date in 29 California schools or districts (Thornton, 1990).

Once a mission and action steps have been agreed to, parents could be invited to join work groups to implement and evaluate school improvement activities.

Developing Plans for School Improvement

Parents could participate in a school improvement council, a task force, an advisory board, or a planning and management team to advise the administration on parental concerns, help review data, and develop plans for improvement. (Suggestions about how to involve parents in decision making will be explored in Chapter 9.)

Obtaining Parents' Perspectives on Personnel Decisions

Parents could participate in the evaluation and hiring of school personnel. Many systems now include parents on search committees for new administrators and invite parents to write to the school board as it is making tenure decisions. Less common is parent participation in hiring teachers or terminating the appointment of an educator. However, parents in the Chicago school system have a majority voice on the local school councils that have the authority to appoint and discharge the principal as well as negotiate the contract and evaluate his or her performance (O'Connell, 1991).

Learning Together

Parents and school personnel could participate in seminars or workshops on topics of mutual interest or concern. Some topics that I know have worked well have been improving parent-teacher conferences, homework, parent involvement, helping children whose parents are separated or divorced, and increasing children's motivation and attention.

Volunteering in the School

Parents' presence in the school contributes resources and support and enhances children's learning, as will be discussed in Chapter 8. Volunteers in the school also help to establish two-way communication. In my experience, as parents learn more about the work that educators do, they become more respectful and admiring of them and more aware of the complex requirements of their roles. As teachers or administrators work directly with parents in collaborative ventures, parents' concerns make more sense and their capacity to contribute in meaningful ways to the ongoing work of the school is continually highlighted. Although seldom anticipated, the opportunity for dialogue, human connection, and mutual appreciation is also extremely beneficial for the adults involved, the children, and the school.

SUMMARY

A fundamental element of home–school partnership is two-way communication. In this chapter, we reviewed ways to establish a culture in which two-way communication is acceptable. We considered both district policy and the roles of principals and teachers in making policy come to life. We also reviewed several approaches schools can use to establish two-way communication, including creating informal opportunities for communication, creating a welcoming atmosphere, clarifying the school's expectations, and developing strategies to hear from parents.

Partnership cannot be forced. The establishment of trust and the conviction that parents and educators are on the same side are not automatic. Regardless of the philosophy that forms the framework for home–school relationships, a judicious selection of suggestions from this chapter should lead to productive interchanges between home and school and foster an interest in further collaboration. Excerpts from interviews with a parent and a teacher who established two-way communication by working together on an advisory board support this point.

> *Teacher*: Participating in the parent-teacher [advisory board] allowed me and some teachers who had never had that experience to realize, "Hey, some parents really care about us as professional people and really are interested

in seeing the school do the best job, and aren't just there to complain. [What works best] is creating channels for continual communication, any structural working together of teachers and parents where the common goal is the betterment of the school. These allow us that working relationship which is not dependent on the child or something where emotions get involved. And that builds nice working relationships. You get to know the adults as adults. You get to feel that we're all on the same side.

Parent: The more opportunities I have to meet with teachers and administrators, the more respectful and more in awe I am of the tremendous job and effort that's done every day, Monday through Friday, and on and on. . . . I feel very accepted as part of a team that is assessing what's good about our schools and where it is that we can become better. . . . And I think that the more parents and teachers share opportunities for helping children, the more trusting we become of one another. And I think the children are the ultimate beneficiaries. (Swap, 1987, pp. 94-95)

In Chapter 6, we will explore how to make conferences between parents and educators the centerpiece of an effective program of two-way communication.

CHAPTER 6

Two-Way Communication During Conferences

In most schools, conferences are the centerpiece of home–school interaction. Of all forms of contact, the child-centered conference is most important to parents and teachers. A statewide survey of working parents in California, for example, found that parents preferred the individual conference to other types of information and programs offered by the school (Hobbs, 1984). Teachers rely on conferences to convey vital information to parents about children's progress and needs.

Even though the parent–teacher conference is the best vehicle we have developed so far for discussing children's progress, it is fraught with problems. For example, many parents do not attend scheduled conferences despite their importance. Epstein's (1987) survey of Maryland school districts, for example, revealed that "more than one-third of the parents had no conferences with the teacher during the year" (p. 124). Although there are many reasons why parents might not attend a scheduled conference, lack of facility with English, child care and transportation problems, or full-time work schedules can be important factors. Sometimes parents do not come because they are not invited. Many urban systems do not offer regularly scheduled conferences.

Another problem is that in many systems, regularly scheduled conferences halt abruptly after elementary school. Junior high school and high school organizations generally do not foster the establishment of individual parent–teacher contacts. However, most parents would still like to find a way to stay in touch with their youngster's school. To illustrate, a recent survey (Dornbusch & Ritter, 1988) indicated that fewer than 20% of all high school parents believed that they should no longer be involved in the education of their children. The survey authors commented that "it is obvious that a reservoir of parental energy and commitment exists that has not been tapped by American high schools" (p. 77).

Perhaps the most fundamental problem with conferences is that even strong, confident, experienced parents and teachers continue to approach conferences with a mixture of hope and dread. As we saw in Chapter 2, teachers and parents invest conferences with enormous symbolic importance. In the best of circumstances, parents and teachers feel that their own skills may be judged by the other. We hope for confirmation and appreciation of the child and of ourselves in our parenting or teaching role: The results are often uninformative or deflating. Of course, if in the past parents or teachers have experienced conferences as punishing, communication can be defensive or angry at the outset. Even without a problem, the brief conference format makes it difficult to develop a working relationship. When there is a problem, the conference format makes it difficult to thoroughly define it, let alone arrive at thoughtful solutions.

Nonetheless, it is worth continuing to invest in the conference format. Some systems have discovered useful adaptations to the traditional structure that result in improvements, and there are many tips for organizing and managing the complex aspects of conferences that help make them more effective. In this chapter, I will review the role of all the key players—administrators, teachers, parents—in making conferences an effective vehicle for home–school collaboration.

The most important goal for the child-centered conference is to orchestrate two-way communication. This means that both teacher and parent(s) or guardian(s) have approximately equal time to share information and express views or concerns; shared expectations are developed; and problem solving and decision making, if needed, are jointly undertaken. Because school personnel are usually in charge of the timing and agenda of the conference, the responsibility for achieving this goal falls primarily on their shoulders.

PREPARATION FOR THE CONFERENCE

What Administrators Can Do

As explained in Chapter 5, principals play a critical role in creating a culture that supports partnership with parents by setting policy, modeling a commitment to parent involvement in their own behavior and attitudes, and facilitating interactions between parents and teachers. Listed below are several specific strategies that principals might consider to improve school–teacher conferences. (Many of these ideas are taken from Braun & Swap, 1987.)

Develop an Appropriate Conference Format and Schedule. Whether conferences occur, when they occur, and how long they take are decisions that are usually made at the district level and shaped by long tradition. Ideally, elementary teachers would have time built into their schedules to meet with every parent twice a year for 15–30 minutes. At the middle and high school levels, a representative of the teaching team or a small team might meet with parents, and the child if desired, once a year. In most schools, this amount of regular contact does not occur because other needs are balanced against the amount of release time allocated for conferences. Such needs might include the level of parent and teacher comfort with the number of days children are released from school, the expense of compensating teachers for evening conferences, and the need to accommodate teacher contract requirements. Balancing the need for regular conferences with these legitimate concerns requires careful negotiation that is best accomplished at the district level.

At the very least, the conditions for conferences should not be so unwieldy that productive conversations cannot occur. A teacher described such a situation to me recently. During an evening devoted to voluntary conferences, eight parents and their small children were all waiting for her in one corner of her classroom while a mother spoke with her. This mother's small child was climbing over the desk, picking up the materials she was trying to show the parent, and occupying much of the mother's attention. The lack of privacy, the distraction and noise of many small children in the room, and the pressure of so many parents waiting for their turn made calm problem solving and sharing impossible. Moreover, since no translators were available, many of the parents, though pleasant and responsive, did not understand the substance of the teacher's remarks.

One strategy for ameliorating such situations is for administrators to put together an ad hoc advisory board of teachers and parents and perhaps community personnel to evaluate whether current conference procedures are working. If there are problems, the group can brainstorm solutions, identify potential resources, and bring these suggestions to the appropriate decision makers: staff (and union representatives), local administration, a school-based management team, or central administration. For example, if child care is a concern, then high school students in a child development class might be recruited, grandparents might be asked to volunteer, and a local video store might donate children's videos for the occasion. Some issues may require a longer time frame for solutions (such as contract requirements), but keeping the overall goal in mind and including teachers and parents in the problem-solving process can create sustained energy for finding solutions.

Underline the Importance of Conferences. Administrators can make clear to parents and teachers through newsletters, staff meetings, and announcements to parents that they think conferences are very important. Allocating always scarce resources to conference periods is one way to signal commitment (e.g., by providing a small budget for such things as refreshments during the conferences, making extra copies of students' materials, providing in-service training and/or release time for teachers). Another way to signal commitment is to send notes to teachers expressing appreciation for hours spent preparing for and participating in conferences.

Administrators can also make clear that conferences are just one way, albeit a very important way, for parents and teachers to work together on behalf of children. They might explain that conferences go better when relationships between parents and teachers already exist, and when a climate of continual collaboration on a variety of issues has been established.

Facilitate Conference Notification. Administrative involvement can facilitate an effective approach to conference notification. Parents are busy and appreciate advance notification of conference appointments. A rule of thumb might be a month's advance notice with a follow-up reminder within a week of the scheduled date.

Some flexibility in conference appointments is ideal. Although many systems are limited in their choices to certain days and times of day for parent–teacher conferences, some parents may not be able to attend unless there are some additional options. Parents appreciate conference requests that are welcoming, personal, and respectful of their importance in the life of the child. If possible, it is good to avoid standardized conference appointment forms with "fill in the blank" spaces for names and times. If standardized forms are a necessity, then a brief personal note from the teacher may make the request less intimidating. Making sure that the notice is written in the family's primary language is a critical step in welcoming participation.

Some systems deal with the problem of many parents and limited conference time by inviting only those parents whose children are not doing well or extending an open invitation to all parents for a particular block of time. Both strategies are flawed. Specifically, if there is a concern about a child, it is best to deal with it when it emerges (rather than waiting until the scheduled conference period). For parents, knowing that they are invited *because* their child is not succeeding makes conference notification a dreaded event, and may breed defensiveness or even apathy. Moreover, inviting all parents or guardians to come at any time during an afternoon or evening time slot is problematic because it is hard for teachers to prepare, and such invitations rarely feel imperative to those parents whose participation requires special encouragement.

Prepare Parents. Parents may have different expectations depending on their backgrounds and history with conferences. Some principals prepare booklets, provide announcements in newsletters, or send letters home explaining the purpose of conferences in school. Such communications could be used to explain what parents might expect, to establish the goal of two-way communication, and to help parents prepare by suggesting that they formulate questions, identify concerns, and share any information that they think might be useful to the teacher.

Offer In-Service to School Personnel. All of us can use practice in listening, delivering and receiving negative information, and resolving conflicts. Regular opportunities to identify and practice "difficult moments" with peer coaching and role playing are also useful. Other useful topics for staff discussions are considering how the conference format itself might work better or how to reach out to parents who do not ordinarily attend conferences. Administrators can initiate occasional systematic evaluation of conference days, where data is collected on who comes, who does not, common themes of concern, aspects that went well, or other specific items.

Act as a Resource to Teachers and Parents. Principals can play many constructive roles to support productive conferences, such as helping parents or teachers to initiate conferences in a timely manner, helping parents or teachers to prepare, acting as a neutral third party, or identifying other appropriate people to participate in conferences when problems are complex.

Teachers often need help in locating appropriate resources for parents who need referrals for physical, emotional, or safety concerns for their families, or for tutorial, enrichment, or other support for their children. Establishing a volunteer team to create an updated resource bank for all school personnel would be an extremely useful administrative contribution.

Provide an Accessible and Comfortable Physical Environment. Sometimes helping parents get to the school is a major concern, particularly in the evening in high crime urban areas or in rural schools that encompass a large geographical area. If some students are bused into the school, then providing the same buses along the same routes for parents can be very helpful. Parents with very low budgets may not be able to afford the cost of public transportation to the school, but a neighborhood carpool might work. Sometimes teachers travel to the neighborhoods where the children live, and use a community agency (library, church building, community center, health clinic) as the setting for conferences (see Freedman, Aschheim, Zerchykov, & Frank, 1989). The initial challenge for the administrator may be to gather data that illuminate what the obstacles to parent participation are as parents perceive them. Then the most appropriate solutions can be developed.

If parents come to the school, the setting should be as welcoming as possible. The recommendations in Chapter 5 for creating a welcoming atmosphere provide general guidelines. In addition, it is wise to help parents who are new to the school find their way to the appropriate classroom, to identify a comfortable setting where parents can wait if necessary, and to provide child care arrangements. The administrator can also support teachers in thinking about how they might best arrange their classrooms to accommodate private adult conversations. In some schools, providing translators is essential.

Enlist the Business Community's Help in Supporting Parent Participation. Administrators can initiate partnerships with businesses to support parent participation in conferences. In Houston, Texas, for example, Operation Fail-Safe enlisted the support of a local advertising firm, which developed a total public awareness campaign. The logo and theme appeared on 100 billboards throughout the city, and approximately $1.7 million was donated in public service advertising by radio, television, and outdoor media. After the first year of operation, parent participation in conferences was up 47%: 75% of elementary parents participated in conferences. The Indianapolis school system adopted and expanded on this idea in its "Parents in Touch" program (Collins, Moles, & Cross, 1982). Businesses can be encouraged to release employees from work for school conference appointments through public awareness campaigns and the endorsement of the idea by a few key business leaders. Some businesses offer work-site seminars to enhance employees' parenting skills.

What Teachers Can Do

Lay the Foundation. Conferences are just one important element in the process of building effective relationships with parents. Finding ways to get to know parents in advance of conferences is very helpful and eases the strain that most of us feel when talking to strangers about important matters. In addition to the suggestions in Chapter 5, some teachers use "half and half" letters to make weekly progress reports to parents and to receive feedback from them. Others use a "positive" telephone program as a way of establishing regular and positive contact, where each parent is given good news about his or her child at least three times a year (see Freedman et al., 1989).

Although it is tempting to postpone all conferences until the regularly scheduled times, some conferences should not wait. If an issue or concern emerges, speaking with parents about it in a timely fashion and in a more flexible format works best.

Make Notification Inviting. Teachers can join with administrators in sending early notification to parents and making it as personal and welcoming as possible. Children could be involved in making covers for invitations, for example, or teachers could append a brief handwritten note to a standardized form. For many parents, hearing from the school means that something is wrong: In contrast, conference notification should be an invitation to partnership.

Awareness of the language backgrounds of parents or guardians is very important, and notification should be translated into parents' primary language to encourage participation. Teachers are most likely to be aware of the family's language background.

Prepare the Environment. Most conferences occur in teachers' classrooms. It is helpful to know who is coming (e.g., mother, father, grandmother, youngster) and plan for seating accordingly. More complicated sometimes is finding another space for other parents and/or children to wait for their appointments. The ideal solution would be to work in conjunction with administrators, other teachers, and perhaps a group of volunteers to arrange for child care and provide a reception area with some light refreshments for adults. Also, some teachers welcome parents in more neutral spaces, such as in church meeting rooms, community centers, or neighborhood agencies.

Prepare for the Conference Itself. There is a lot of preparation required to use conference time wisely. For routinely scheduled conferences, most teachers review children's work and assemble a judicious selection for parents' viewing. It is also useful for teachers to select a few key issues they want to discuss with parents or guardians in the limited time available. They might want to jot down a few anecdotes or converse with other teachers to gather additional information.

It makes sense to develop an agenda for each conference and then to set priorities, assuming that half of the available meeting time will be devoted to parents' questions, concerns, or ideas. Calculating approximately how much time would be needed to discuss a particular issue is a useful first step in setting realistic priorities and helps prevent a frantic listing of the remaining issues in the last 2 minutes of allotted time. If necessary, a follow-up conference could be scheduled. The most important principle in setting priorities is to remember that the overall goal of the conference is to establish a year-long partnership with the parent or guardian. Therefore, attending to the development of a trusting relationship is essential.

Teachers can also alert principals to the needs parents may have for translation so that the appropriate language specialists can be available at the conference site. Because of issues of status and confidentiality, it is best not to use children or neighbors as translators, but professional translators or students from a local university might be appropriate alternatives. There are important skills to learn in using translators, such as waiting for the translator to consider how to frame the conversation in each language and adapting one's conversation style to correspond to the educational background of the family member. For further information on planning conferences with families with limited English proficiency, see Appendix D.

What Parents Can Do

Get Involved. Parents also need to know that conferences tend to go better when relationships between teachers and parents have already been established. Ideally, parents will take advantage of ways of getting to know the teacher by participating in events or contributing to the school prior to scheduled conferences. If work or family commitments make coming to school during the day difficult, parents or guardians might write notes to the teacher, call, or volunteer to help out on class projects over the weekend or in the evening.

Don't Wait. If an issue or concern arises and scheduled conferences seem a long way off, parents should not wait. A chat on the telephone or an individually scheduled conference when a problem first emerges may prevent a full-blown crisis later on.

Be Prepared. For parents, being prepared may mean assembling relevant assessment records, collecting information about certain behaviors of concern, trying to define an issue in a clear and compelling way, or simply trying to clear one's mind prior to the conference. Just as for teachers, it may be helpful for parents or guardians to make a list of issues or concerns and then to set priorities, knowing that time will be short.

In my experience as a parent and as a teacher, it is most helpful if parents come to a conference with a clear definition of a problem, but not with a particular solution. Arriving at a conference with one and only one solution that a teacher is supposed to implement usually elicits defensiveness and may prevent the joint discovery of an even better solution.

Attend the Conference. Even though conferences may be an imperfect mechanism for communication, they offer an opportunity to begin to develop a working relationship with a child's teacher. If the scheduled appointment is not convenient, parents can request another or make a telephone appointment. Not attending a conference poses risks because, unfortunately, teachers often interpret parents' failure to attend as a signal of their not caring about the child or the school.

TIPS FOR CONDUCTING CONFERENCES

Setting the Stage

Ideally, a teacher and parent will be able to set a tentative agenda for the conference and establish a good working relationship within the first minute or two of conversation.

Establishing an Agenda. When the moment of truth arrives, the teacher traditionally has the responsibility for setting the tone and establishing the format of the conference. After trying to put the parent at ease, some teachers spend the first few minutes outlining their agenda and asking parents whether they have particular issues they want to discuss. Then a tentative agenda is agreed to. At a minimum, expressing a commitment to sharing the time with the parent and then doing so are very important.

From the parents' perspective, if the teacher does not provide an initial opportunity to set an agenda, the parents should speak up rather than waiting until the end of the conference. For example, a parent might simply say, "I'd like to be sure we save time to talk about how Jim is getting along with the other children." Often such a request prompts both parties to develop a timetable, or the concern is immediately discussed.

In the context of establishing an agenda, I have often found that the ritual of going over a report card or examining a work folder can be a distraction from more important issues. Often the entire time allotted for the conference is used up in reviewing the material. Such a format suggests that the only important information to share about the child is revealed by grades or work papers, and this is generally not the case. I have found that both teacher and parent often feel that in devoting their time to this agenda, they are responding to the other's wishes (though not their own), but this mutual misperception rarely becomes explicit. Some teachers have found a solution to this problem by giving the parent(s) or guardian the child's work folder to review a few days before the conference or while parents wait to speak to the teacher.

Appreciating the Child's Unique Qualities. Many parents have told me that the bottom line for them in any dialogue with the teacher is to find out whether the teacher knows and appreciates their child. Research also confirms that parents value conferences with teachers not only to gain information about their child, but also to assess the teacher's understanding of the child (Hauser-Cram, 1983). Parents hope that the teacher recognizes and appreciates the uniqueness of their child. Hauser-Cram quotes a parent she interviewed whose views were representative.

> Anything in this day and age that lets you know that your child is recognized as a unique person in that classroom and eligible for anything beyond purely ordinary consideration is amazingly impressive to a parent. Any unique feature your child has, whether they're funny . . . or whether they have an unflagging interest in worms . . . just the whole idea of the child being special and unique is important. (p. 10)

Hauser-Cram continues:

> Parents used teacher's knowledge of their child's personality or interests as a screening device . . . a means of determining whether or not they were going to grant the teacher credibility. If they decided that a teacher did, in fact, appreciate their child's uniqueness, then they were much more willing to value a teacher's comments about the child's academic skills and even impressions that may not be entirely positive. (pp. 111–112)

The implications for teachers are clear. It is wise to include not only a discussion of data that would measure the child against others, but also an anecdote or two that communicates a vivid picture of the uniqueness of the child. Parents can be reassured by just a sentence or two, such as retelling a joke that Peter told the class, or mentioning that Jane shared half her sandwich when Mary forgot hers, or describing precisely what happens when John loses his concentration.

Trying to capture the child's uniqueness is a more useful way of connecting to a parent or guardian than sharing "one nice thing." Parents tell me they are not often reassured by comments like, "Jane is such a lovely girl," or "Bob has so much energy," even if they are well intentioned. Parents who have been through many conferences have even told me that they dread hearing the "good thing" first, because they know that the "bad thing" is bound to follow, and they just wait for the "other shoe to drop."

Appreciating the Teacher's Professional Role. Just as parents seek assurance that the teacher understands the child's uniqueness, teachers respond more favorably to parents who appreciate the complexities they face in trying to meet the needs of a large group of children. A quote from Hauser-Cram's (1983) interviews with teachers illustrates this point.

> I think that, yes, they have to understand that we are professionals, that my time is valuable, that I'm not here to serve one parent or one child. But that I must work with 20-something groups of parents. And that it's very difficult, sometimes, to get to every little thing they ask you to do. Having them keep that as a frame of reference. (p. 129)

Thus, parents would be wise to acknowledge the realities of the teacher's responsibilities. For example, "I have enough trouble trying to divide my attention among my three kids. It's hard to imagine how you teach 25!" Such recognition does not prevent parents from advocating for their child, but it may help to assure the teacher that the parents' expectations will not be unreasonable.

Using Effective Communication Skills

Generally conferences do not require a sophisticated level of communication skills. Parent–teacher exchanges are typically pleasant and matter-of-fact. However, disagreements do occur. The conferences that loom in the minds of teachers, parents, and administrators with whom I work are those where disagreements become personal attacks, where a judgment about the child was made with which they violently disagreed, or where a course of action was recommended or taken that they thought was dead wrong.

If you are unfamiliar with these kinds of stories, let me mention three recent examples. (1) An African-American mother described to me the feelings of outrage and helplessness that were evoked in her during a conference with her daughter's teacher. The teacher was recommending her daughter for placement in a special education class, yet she felt that her daughter was bright and capable and that the teacher was seriously misjudging her daughter's abilities. (2) A principal described his chagrin at getting into a shouting match with a parent during a conference. The parent came to complain about the first-grade teacher's lesson on the family, which she felt was an invasion of privacy. The parent denounced the teacher and threatened to go to the superintendent and the school committee. The principal lost his patience because he did not agree with the mother's evaluation of the lesson and because he resented being threatened. (3) A teacher described her anger during a conference when a parent insisted that the curriculum was not challenging enough and her child was bored.

When time is short and the issues are important, it takes practiced skill to cope with the feelings that such conflicts generate and to nonetheless negotiate decisions that are mutually agreeable. Administrators, teachers, and parents must use all the communication skills they possess to continue to collaborate when sharp differences of opinion arise. The suggestions that are given here present some guidelines in helping to listen, give and receive negative feedback, and negotiate differences in an atmosphere of respect, even when one feels personally or professionally challenged.

Listening. There are several things that make listening difficult. One of them is the need that many parents and teachers feel to maintain the protective stance described in Chapter 3. If collaboration and open discussion of conflict are not normative, then it is difficult for individuals to risk authentic listening and sharing. When a problem does not go away and needs to be resolved, then the comfort of the Protective model breaks down. The lack of authentic dialogue that is characteristic of the Protective model is often counterproductive in these situations and can make parents (or teachers) very angry and mistrustful. For example, the mother in a previous example who thought her daughter's abilities were being misjudged also felt that the teacher was not listening to her evidence and objections. Her dissatisfaction at not being heard was expressed as "being worked over by the system." She was deeply concerned not only about a misdiagnosis but also by her conviction that no real exchange was taking place. Overcoming the normative barrier that inhibits careful listening and exchange requires individual and group commitment to an interactive model of home–school communication.

Physical constraints such as exhaustion or illness, or psychological constraints such as anxiety over waiting children or competing appointments can limit our ability to concentrate on the speaker's messages. An important step in effective listening is to create a context for conversation in which both parties can feel reasonably prepared and relaxed. In my experience, teachers (and parents) do not often recognize that they have some choice in arranging the circumstances of a conference. A parent dropping by and asking for time need not be seen immediately if the teacher is not prepared or is not feeling well. A teacher (or parent) need not stay in a conversation that has become demeaning or abusive. The teacher (or parent) can respectfully state the problem, arrange for another time, and terminate the conference.

Increasingly, listening is made more complicated by differences in background that make it difficult to correctly interpret the meaning of another's verbal and nonverbal messages. Differences in background are especially difficult to evaluate because one may not even note them consciously or recognize that accurate communication has not taken place. For example, cultural patterns dictate such nonverbal behaviors as the appropriate physical distance between two persons, the meaning of eye contact, the appropriateness of touch, and respectful postures. Cultures may also dictate the structure of verbal exchanges, such as who should initiate conversation, whether interruption is acceptable, the expected time between a question and its answer, and whether and how to bring up problems. If these rhythms are not automatically shared, listening partners may feel uncomfortable or alienated but not understand the source of their discomfort. Consider this illustration:

> Scollon and Scollon's (1981) lengthy analyses of inter-ethnic conversations among Athabaskan Indians and whites in Alaska reveal that something as simple as a shift in rhythm between speakers can lead to personal judgments of a speaker's capabilities. For example, a white speaker often will ask a question, then pause, waiting for the Indian speaker to reply; then, when it appears the listener has nothing to say, the white speaker will speak again. The Indian, who wishes to reply, but is accustomed to longer pauses between speakers, is not given an adequate opportunity to speak.
>
> On the other hand, when Indian speakers do have the floor, they are interrupted frequently because they take what are perceived by whites to be "lengthy" pauses between thoughts. As an Athabaskan woman said to one of us, "While you're thinking about what you're going to say, they're already talking." Hence, Indian speakers often say very little and white speakers seem to do all the talking. (Nelson-Barber & Meier, 1990, p. 3)

In addition to cultural differences in speech and conversational patterns, values underlying children's learning may also not be shared. For example, how adults express their authority, reinforce children, and support independence vary significantly across cultures (for additional cultural context variables, see Delpit, 1986, 1988; Irujo, 1989; Nelson-Barber & Meier, 1990; Yao, 1985).

Becoming alert to all of these messages is part of careful listening. If an educator's background has not included a study of the cultures of the students in his or her class and school, then the solution is to learn more about these patterns alone or in conjunction with colleagues through reading, consultation, direct experience, and/or coursework; or to work in teams with individuals to whom the patterns are familiar. Finally, it is hard to listen in a conflict situation because feelings of defensiveness and reciprocal anger lead us to try to justify our position and to make "fight or flight" responses.

One can learn the skill of listening nondefensively (just as one can learn the skill of delivering one's own opinion clearly). There are skills we can practice to be good listeners in difficult moments, such as keeping silent (with occasional reinforcement for the speaker, such as "Uh-huh," or "I see"), clarifying messages that one does not understand, or paraphrasing conversations to check understanding and provide a summary of the exchange. (See Brammer, 1988, for definitions of each skill and transcripts illustrating examples of each in a counseling context. Appendix E contains a transcript of an exchange between a teacher and a parent who are struggling over a difficult problem, where the teacher demonstrates excellent listening skills.)

The bottom line is that listening is fundamental to achieving a partnership, and that two-way communication, not just speaking our own message, is the goal of an effective conference. From the teacher's perspective, taking time to learn about the cultures of the children in his or her classes and practicing listening skills are therefore worth the effort. From the parent's perspective also, practicing communication skills with other parents to prepare for a difficult conference can be beneficial to the child, as can meeting with other more experienced parents to learn the "ways of doing things" in the school.

Giving Negative Information. There are two important components of giving negative information: preparation and delivery. To prepare, one must think through priorities (what is essential; what can be postponed until another meeting; how much will the parent [or teacher] be able to absorb in one setting). Gathering anecdotes, observing the child, and thinking through how one will express the information are additional steps.

In delivering negative information, it works best to describe one's own experiences and feelings in specific terms, providing examples or citing specific, observable behaviors. The goal is to paint a picture so that the recipient has a clear, compelling idea of what is happening. The corollary is to avoid blaming, generalizations, or negative judgments. Working to paint a picture also helps one to avoid labels and complex educational jargon.

One should ask for and then listen to reactions to the negative information that one has delivered. A rule of thumb is to offer only a few sentences before seeking a reaction. The recipient needs to have time and space to reflect, see if the data match his or her experience, clarify information, and ask questions.

Because giving negative information is so hard for most of us, we tend to speak in paragraphs, justifying our conclusions to the last detail. In the case of negative information being delivered to parents about a child, this strategy often leaves parents feeling overwhelmed by the data and convinced that the teacher sees nothing of value in their child. At the opposite extreme are those of us who find delivering negative information so distasteful that we save it to the end of the conference or explain the data in such a kind and tactful way that the message is neither delivered nor received. Ideally, the information delivered will emerge as a clear statement of a problem, which the teacher and parent(s) and child can then work on solving together over time—and not necessarily during the conference at hand if the information requires digestion.

Receiving Negative Information. It is difficult for teachers (or parents) to receive negative information about a student's lack of progress or an aspect of classroom practice. In these situations, however, the first skill is to learn to acknowledge the concern and establish a mutually agreeable time and place to talk about it. Once the conference is underway, the goal is for the recipient of the negative information to listen, asking for specific examples, anecdotes, or behavioral examples in order to fully understand the concern. Trying to determine the speaker's feelings and his or her goals and hopes for the communication are also important. (Does she want something to change? Does he want you to understand how he feels?)

Though it is very tempting, it is best if the recipient of feedback does not respond defensively or take the feedback personally. Preferable options are to acknowledge and accept the concerns expressed, share one's own point of view, engage in mutual problem solving, or take time to reflect on what one has heard and schedule another meeting.

Avoiding Impasse and Resolving Conflicts. As partnerships deepen, differences of opinion and strategy inevitably will arise. The fact that parents and school personnel feel trusting enough to raise differences openly can be a very positive sign, but it is also useful to establish some ground rules so that disputes do not fester but get resolved. (The ground rules explained below are adapted from Braun & Swap, 1987.)

The first three steps in resolving disputes are by now familiar: arrange to discuss the issue as soon as possible; share information and feelings clearly and vividly; listen to the other's point of view. Next, see if it is possible to agree on a definition of the problem. If parents and school personnel see the same things and share the same degree of concern, then it is possible to work on developing solutions.

If there is disagreement about the nature of the problem, then try to further clarify what each is seeing and experiencing by asking for further examples. If disagreement persists, there are several options.

1. *Analyze your feelings and rethink your position.* What factors are influencing your feelings on the issue? Has the problem become the focus for a power struggle? What is in the best interests of the child?
2. *Try to understand the other's point of view.* Why might the parent (or teacher) take this point of view? What are his or her possible interests? (Interests are what cause a person to take a position.)
3. *Check out your own perceptions with a trusted friend or colleague who is honest with you.* What insights can you gain?
4. *Arrange to meet again.* If you plan to bring someone else with you, state that in advance, and make all written communications as friendly and unthreatening as possible.
5. *Negotiate.* Try to avoid holding onto one and only one solution to a complex problem. Instead, try to identify each side's interests, any common interests, and the relative importance of each interest to each side. See if it is possible to negotiate a solution that adequately meets the most important needs of each partner, and be prepared to compromise.
6. *Involve a mediator.* If unable to resolve the dispute together, then seek the help of a neutral third party or some higher authority. Do this calmly and firmly, without threats and hostility. (For an extended discussion of resolving conflicts, see Fisher & Ury, 1981.)

To illustrate, the principal in the earlier example had not learned why the mother was concerned about the lesson on the family. Why she felt that the lesson intruded on the family's privacy was never explored. The fact that differences in her husband's cultural background affected her judgments and compelled her "interests" in resisting this lesson had not occurred to the principal, nor had she felt inclined to share this information with him. Neither was successful in communicating his or her point of view vividly, and neither understood the other's concerns or underlying interests. Because both were so angry, neither the principal nor the mother sought help from trusted colleagues to try to gain insight into their conflict; instead, both sought confirmation from others that their "opponent" was in the wrong. This led the principal to believe that partnership with parents was impossible; training in conflict resolution might have provided him with additional skills that would have defused the incident and led to increased mutual understanding.

Summary. Teachers and parents are rarely taught communication skills. Though not foolproof, the guidelines offered above are useful under most conditions. The best way to learn them is to practice the skills by role-playing "difficult" situations, with colleagues to coach and support the effort. When staff members have been through this experience together, they can also be helpful to each other in preparing for or gaining insight into real situations.

Although these skills are presented in the context of individual parent–teacher conferences, they are also useful for group decision making, as in a school-based management team. Ideally, the school or system also will make it possible for teachers and parents to learn these skills so that individual and group problem solving will be more efficient, effective, and nonthreatening.

COMMON CHALLENGES IN ESTABLISHING TWO-WAY COMMUNICATION

Parents of Children with Special Needs

Parents of children with special needs are required by law to meet with school personnel to make decisions about their children's placement and program. Federal legislation (Public Law 94–142) requires active parent participation on at least an annual basis in all decisions made about a child's Individual Educational Plan (IEP).

A lengthening body of research literature confirms that IEP conferences are often not good examples of two-way communication (e.g., Brinckerhoff & Vincent, 1986; Turnbull & Turnbull, 1990). Parents often are the recipients of negative information about their child; they frequently feel intimidated by the array of teachers, specialists, and administrators who attend the meetings with them; and they are rarely equal partners in decision making. For example, Brinckerhoff and Vincent (1986) cited several studies that demonstrated that IEPs were often developed by school staff before the meeting, and that teachers ranked parental contributions as less important than their own. Moreover, many school staff members had negative attitudes about the IEP process, believing that it was too demanding of their time and irrelevant to daily instruction.

Those authors believed that effective use of the IEP as an opportunity for collaboration had been inhibited by lack of knowledge, tradition, and experience about how to share information fully and negotiate differences when participants were not equally powerful. Therefore, they developed a process of parent and staff training that increased parental decision making during IEP conferences. Parents were taught how to write a developmental assessment and developmental profile, how to participate in the meeting, and how to establish their own priorities. Staff members were given summaries of the parents' assessments and were asked to listen to parents' goals and concerns before presenting their own. "Statistical analyses indicated a significantly greater frequency in contributions, goals generated, and programming decisions made at IEP meetings by the experimental group" (Brinckerhoff & Vincent, 1986, p. 46).

The principles underlying the guidelines for preparing for and conducting parent-teacher conferences also apply to IEP conferences. However, for an IEP conference, it might be necessary to allocate at least 45 minutes; attention to clear notification is even more important because the federal requirements are very specific; and a welcoming physical environment can lessen anxiety. In addition, many systems appoint a parent liaison to talk with parents before and after the meeting. This coordinator can ascertain parents' preferences about meeting conditions and determine if parents have any information needs or concerns. The coordinator could also prepare parents or guardians for the meeting by explaining what to expect, how to prepare, what their rights are, and that the school is interested in their views. The team's conference time can then be focused more productively, and the decisions are likely to be of better quality. If school personnel have not yet considered appointing a liaison, then parents may wish to request access to a specific person to help them prepare for the meeting.

Negotiating priorities for the student's IEP is a particularly critical element of this conference. Including the student in the conference whenever possible is useful to ascertain his or her needs, goals, and priorities for learning. Identifying parents' priorities and their interest in and availability to take responsibility for teaching some of the objectives is very important, since often this involvement is simply taken for granted.

Taking time to explain the results of the conference to the student, speaking with key staff who were not present but are part of the implementation team, and making a written record of conference decisions are necessary parts of post-conference follow-up for IEP conferences. Because there are usually several people involved, an oral and written summary of who agreed to do what and when is usually helpful, along with specific strategies for maintaining communication and monitoring any tentative decisions.

Another serious concern of parents and educators is that children of color are overidentified as having special needs. For example, Chinn and Hughes (1987) reported that the percentage of black children in classes for the educable mentally retarded was 48.30% as compared with 24.52% in total school enrollment. Hispanics were overrepresented in Arizona and New Mexico in classes for the retarded and learning disabled; Native Americans were overrepresented in classes for the learning disabled. The concern is that there are patterns of attitudes and practices among educators (such as tracking and overreferral to special education) that are not supportive of the achievement of children from diverse backgrounds. Critics assert that the problems are incorrectly located in the children rather than in the system that we have developed for educating them (Comer, 1988a; Davies, 1988; Hopfenberg et al., 1990; Wheelock, 1990).

It is understandable that the difficulties of accepting a diagnosis and a special placement would be made much more complex for parents who believed that educators' judgments were influenced by bias, low expectations, or uninspired educational methods. Although clearly a very complex issue, solutions are most likely to be found in a school that adopts a Partnership model for achieving success for all children, as described in Chapter 4. The combination of responsive curriculum and instructional practices, innovative structures for identifying and resolving student and staff problems (such as Comer's Student Staff Services Team), and partnership between home and school to reduce educational discontinuities are most likely to reduce overreferral of children of color.

"Hard to Reach" Parents

The problem with the label "hard to reach" is that the difficulty in establishing communication is placed on the parents rather than on the methods educators have developed to reach out. My research (Swap, 1990c) suggests that even "hard to reach" parents are not so hard to reach when they are offered programs that are respectful of their strengths and backgrounds, responsive to their needs, and scheduled at times and places that they can manage.

The first step in reaching out is to try to determine who is not coming to conferences and why. Is it parents of low-achieving children, parents who do not speak English, parents whose cultures do not identify parent involvement as a priority, parents from a particular ethnic or racial group within the school, teen-age parents, parents with extensive work schedules, parents who live far from the school, parents who are poor or without homes, middle-class parents?

Once this information has been collected, outreach strategies need to be adopted that will address the underlying issues. For example, are non-English speaking parents and homeless parents receiving and understanding conference requests? Is the timing for conferences sufficiently flexible to accommodate parents with extensive work schedules or is it possible to communicate with them through other formats, such as home visits or telephone contacts? If some parents are feeling alienated or embarrassed about coming to school, are there neighbors or friends who are already involved or respected figures within the community who might be used as liaisons? If getting to the school is too expensive or dangerous for some parents, could a closer, more familiar location be selected or transportation be provided by the school?

The keys to multiplying the level of parent involvement in a school are as follows: to really believe in its importance; to collect data that will help to isolate the problems; and to devote systematic planning, creativity, and resources to addressing problems. Often, the same strategies do not work for each subgroup. Therefore, the initial goal may not be to bring everybody together to do the same activities, but to establish initial contacts with each subgroup and to begin to develop a strategy for building trust in each that will bear fruit over time.

"Over-involved" Parents

Teachers are fearful of being swallowed up by parents who demand too much of their time with telephone calls, unplanned conferences, and requests for appointments. They can also be resentful of parents who they feel have not learned to "let go" of their child or his or her education, and who demonstrate that by failing to listen to or accept the teacher's judgments and recommendations about the child's academic, social, and emotional growth.

One problem in making suggestions about this issue is that educators do not agree on what constitutes over-involvement. Individual tolerances are very different: One teacher's pest can be another's thoughtful partner.

As we have seen, school norms also differ about what constitutes "too much" parent involvement.

If we assume, though, that there are some parents who do seem to struggle hard with "letting go," here are some guidelines. Teachers are more secure about responding to parental requests if they receive support from the administration in doing so, such as having a scheduled time during the school day for telephone calls and a private place to make them; support from the principal for placing reasonable restrictions on parents' access to their time out of school; money for stationery and stamps; and a support team, preferably on-site, for discussing difficult situations.

In my experience, parents often arrive at this point because of a traumatic history in dealing with professionals or their child. For example, if the child is prone to life-threatening allergic attacks or has been seriously misdiagnosed or poorly taught, it can be hard for parents to feel brave enough or supported enough to trust professionals again. The best strategy is to listen to the parents' story and to try to get to the heart of the concern. Often, this is the last thing educators want to do, because they are already feeling that the parent has taken too much of their time. Nonetheless, this strategy often saves time in the long run. It provides the educator with a deeper understanding, often some sympathy for the parents' reality, and, therefore, usually a better idea about how to help. Moreover, the experience of being sympathetically listened to generally builds the parents' confidence in the educator and lessens their worries about their child. Sometimes educators can supplement their own careful listening with outside resources. A referral to a counselor, an invitation to a parent support group, or an invitation to become actively involved in some aspect of the school that does not directly involve the child may be useful to some parents if sensitively suggested.

Another version of over-involvement that is very distressing to teachers occurs when parents offer teachers advice about how or what to teach. The concern is often not the content of the recommendation, but the disrespect for the teacher's professionalism that is conveyed by the parent. The level of annoyance is often exaggerated when the parent is of a higher status in the community than the teacher. Although not foolproof solutions, two strategies are to provide multiple channels to enable the parent to gather information about educational goals and the reasons for them, and to invite such parents to participate constructively in school-based evaluation and decision making. Participation of such parents on a School Improvement Council or as volunteers in the classroom often elicits greater respect in them for the complexity of the teacher's role as well as some ownership of curriculum choices.

SUMMARY

Establishing two-way communication in conferences is critical to successful parent involvement. Conferences are the most important and consistent communication activity in schools. Nonetheless, parents often do not attend conferences or participate actively, and both parents and teachers face them with a mixture of dread and hope.

This chapter has explained what parents, teachers, and administrators can do to prepare for and participate in two-way conferences. The basic ingredients of key communication skills were also discussed, including listening, giving and receiving negative information, and conflict resolution.

Some attention was devoted to IEP conferences, since these are even more difficult to manage than the parent–teacher conference in terms of complexity of content and numbers of players. Finally, the school's role in de-labeling and reaching out to "hard to reach" and "over-involved" parents was discussed.

CHAPTER 7

Enhancing Children's Learning at Home and School

The primary purpose of a partnership between home and school is to support and enhance children's learning. Ideally a child should know that his or her parents or guardian and the teacher are on the "same side," as reflected in continuity of expectations, frequent exchange of information, and explicit mutual support. Moreover, children's learning is enhanced if parents and teachers use an array of complementary strategies to contribute to their learning and development. In this chapter, I will explore two major avenues for home–school collaboration to support children's learning: parent involvement in children's learning at school, and creating a culture at home that supports school success.

PARENT INVOLVEMENT IN CHILDREN'S LEARNING AT SCHOOL

The literature on parent involvement and children's school achievement that was reviewed in Chapter 1 made it clear that parent involvement in school activities increased student achievement as long as that involvement was comprehensive, long-lasting, and well planned. Schools with higher levels of parent involvement had higher student achievement profiles even in low-income areas. The type of involvement was not a critical variable. Apparently, however, parent involvement does not always need to be comprehensive to contribute to the achievement of individual students. For example, a survey of 7,836 students and their parents and teachers at six San Francisco Bay Area high schools indicated that parental attendance at high school events (Open School Night, College Night, athletic events) was related to higher student grades (Dornbusch & Ritter, 1988). This finding held regardless of parents' level of education or social class. The authors asked parents to help them explain this finding.

> Some parents said their attendance at school events actively demonstrated the values they express verbally to their children. By taking the time and

trouble to spend an evening at school, they were showing the sincerity of their emphasis on education. Others remarked that they were better able to communicate with their children after having observed some aspects of the world in which their children spend so much of the day. If their children gave distorted reports of events at school, they were better able to support teachers after having gone to the school and judged the situation for themselves. (p. 76)

Although this study does not offer evidence of the generalizability of this relationship in other communities or grade levels, it is suggestive of the potential power of parent behaviors and attitudes to shape youngsters' motivation to succeed in school. While even minimum levels of parent involvement at school may influence children's achievement, some types of parent involvement programs at school are particularly promising because of their ingenuity or potential for supporting increased levels of partnership (and children's learning) over time. In this section, examples are provided of parent activities in school that support children's learning. Though not exhaustive, they illustrate basic principles for activity development and implementation.

Parents as Tutors in School

Parents can be very effective in supporting children's learning at school in the role of tutors, aides, or volunteers. Whether parents help individual or small groups of children with assignments, read aloud to small groups of children, help children to select appropriate literature in the library, or assist in computer-based instruction, tutors extend what schools can accomplish. Children benefit from the increased individualization of instruction; additional resources of knowledge, time, and nurturance; and (as mentioned in Chapter 3), the reduction of dissonance between home and school.

Lightfoot (1978) reported on many benefits of working in the school as seen by a group of mothers working in the Liberty School.

The mothers reported that many behavioral and learning problems in school seemed to disappear when 1) their child experienced an alliance between mother and teacher; 2) they were able to help teachers become more perceptive and responsive to the needs of their children; 3) their participation in classroom life helped to reduce the workload of teachers; 4) they were able to directly perceive and fully comprehend the complexities and burdensome nature of the teaching role; 5) they could teach some of the teachers, who were not parents, something about nurturance and mothering; 6) they were able to perceive of the school as belonging to them. (pp. 173–174)

My own research at P.S. 111 in New York City confirmed these results (Swap, 1990c). A group of 12 Latino parents who had been active in the school for 2 years as tutors and volunteers had many positive benefits to report. For example, they learned what was expected of their children by the teacher, discovered how they could be really useful at school, connected more easily to teachers who now came to them if they had concerns about their children, became more involved with reading to their children at home, and saw many specific examples of growth in their own children's learning and self-esteem. They also gave several examples of how they contributed to the learning of children who were not their own and how they felt they were contributing to positive changes for the whole school by advocating for additional classroom resources and an after-school program. They explained that they now understood more about how teachers felt when in the classroom. As one mother summarized: "We keep learning with them."

A teacher in the same school provided a complementary perspective of the importance of a family presence in school. She said: "It's the children of parents who are usually around who excel. Teachers are more attentive to their children because parents are keeping a close eye on them." She added that these parents had extended themselves for her and helped her a lot. (For additional information, see Swap, 1990c.)

Including parents in the school as tutors is generally the culmination of a long process of negotiation and building relationships between parents and educators. Particularly when there is dissonance between the cultures of the home and school, teachers fear the disruption that parents might cause, as this teacher from an urban elementary school asserts.

> This sounds terrible, but . . . some parents are low-skilled and illiterate. Such parents would have to be willing to accept correction. Parents should not be permitted to bring their toddlers into the classrooms, and parents would have to refrain from drinking alcohol and smoking if they chose to work in the classroom.

If teachers' and parents' fears of each other can be overcome and a program is initiated, the program must be well coordinated for the tutorial help to be predictable and maximally useful for teachers. A coordinator can identify parent interests and availability, establish teachers' needs, match teachers and tutors, arrange training (centrally or through individual teachers), and monitor the program. The coordinator may be a teacher or parent (volunteer or paid) or a representative of a larger citywide volunteer association. A procedure for celebrating and publicly acknowledging tutors' contributions is also important. Tutors may be volunteers or paid aides.

When tutorial programs are well coordinated, teachers often feel, as this teacher explained in an interview, that "I don't understand how we ever got along without the parents' help." An unanticipated benefit of parents' involvement in the school is that the experience often leads to new opportunities for parents, such as the pursuit of more advanced education for themselves or being hired in educational roles. (For additional information, see National School Volunteer Program, 1979; South Carolina State Department of Education, 1985; or contact the National Association of Partners in Education in Alexandria, Virginia.)

Parents as Contributors to Curriculum Development

Extensively described in Chapter 3, parent involvement in researching, developing, selecting, or sharing curriculum is a very important way for parents to be involved in enhancing their own children's learning as well as contributing to the pedagogical and social culture of the school.

Parents as Mentors

Schools are increasingly taking advantage of parental experience in professions, hobbies, or avocations to enrich learning opportunities for youngsters throughout the grades. Parents' help may be sought based on educators' awareness of their skills, or all parents or guardians might be asked to fill out a questionnaire describing their expertise, interests, and willingness to participate in school (e.g., amount of time they might contribute; willingness to bring children to their work site; preferences for topic or age group). A brief note to acknowledge parents' willingness to participate is an important trust-building step, even if they are not invited to school immediately.

Armed with this information, school personnel may request that parents be involved (for example) in supervising a youngster's independent project, coming to school to discuss their own careers, or sponsoring a high school youngster in an apprenticeship program.

One interesting variant of the mentor concept was a program developed to extend students' understanding of their local communities in conjunction with an eighth-grade social studies curriculum. As Freedman, Aschheim, Zerchykov, & Frank (1990) outlined the program:

> Through a "Town Government Program," students get to know how their town works from first hand experience. Parents who work in various offices and on volunteer boards make presentations in classrooms several times each semester. This program is integrated into the children's social studies curriculum and encourages civic responsibility through presenting many options for civic involvement. Participating speakers attempt to give students the total picture of adult citizenship; they indicate that they not only work at a job but also find other ways to contribute to their communities through volunteer positions. (p. 54)

Community mentors also supplement children's learning. For example, P.S. 146 in New York City provides a Models for Success program, where adults from the community or similar neighborhoods who achieved success "against the odds" share information about their own lives (Clinchy, 1992).

Parents' Involvement in Mini-Grant Programs

An innovative idea developed by the Schools Reaching Out project (Krasnow, 1990b) provided an incentive for teachers to experiment with having parents directly involved with students' learning. Through outside funding, mini-grants of $200 per teacher (up to $3,000 each for two schools) were offered to teachers to use in any way they chose as long as parents were included in the plan. More than half the teachers in each school took advantage of the opportunity. Teachers used the funds in varied ways. For example, two teachers used the mini-grants to pay for a field trip. Parents were invited to plan the trip, accompany the class, and follow up with reading and writing projects at home. An art teacher asked parents to join her in helping children do research on the uses of masks in several cultures and then to assist children in producing their own masks at school. Two primary teachers worked together with parents to plan and stock an early learning resource center for children and families.

Teachers, parents, and children evaluated these projects very favorably. For teachers who were not accustomed to parent involvement in school, this format allowed them to simultaneously enrich their curriculum and establish a new level of involvement with parents with which they felt comfortable.

CREATING A CULTURE AT HOME THAT SUPPORTS
SCHOOL SUCCESS

Parents today often find it difficult to figure out how to contribute to the development of a healthy, happy, successful child. They are more likely now than in the past to have fewer resources on which to draw in gathering ideas and reassurance about their parenting practices. Parents of young children often live far away from their families of origin; mothers' and fathers' work schedules may make it more difficult to be involved in a peer support network; in many parts of the country there is less of a sense of "neighborhood" than formerly. It may also be hard for parents to try to replicate the strategies that their parents used in raising them, since family circumstances today are very different from even 2 decades ago. Moreover, child development experts in each of the last 3 decades have offered conflicting advice to parents about such topics as setting limits and the best ways of supporting children's learning.

To help fill this vacuum, national, state, and local education and parent organizations and often local schools have created an array of resource materials and parent education opportunities. The resources suggested below are organized into three categories to clarify the different ways that parents can support their child's learning at home. In addition, I discuss special issues for parents of color and ways that parents can offer support to each other.

Meeting Children's Basic Needs

Most parent groups and educational authorities agree that children's learning is supported when parents make sure that children get sufficient rest, are fed an ample and nutritious diet, get to school regularly and on time, are dressed appropriately for the weather, have clean clothes to wear, and have a quiet and well-lit place to work at home.

Single-page handouts are available for parents that make these points. For example, the Office of Educational Research and Improvement in the Department of Education in Washington, D.C., has a handout available called "Help Your Child Improve in Test-Taking" (no date) that reviews most of these ideas. Local early childhood programs and elementary schools sometimes offer workshops to parents on nutrition, needs of children at different "ages and stages," and how to cope with children's sleeping or eating problems. The goals of these activities are to share information, help parents talk about and work through common problematic issues, and create a useful support network for parents.

When parents do not have the financial resources to purchase appropriate clothes, wash them regularly, or provide their children with nourishing food, schools have options. A school in Philadelphia, for example, has installed a washing machine and dryer. Local merchants donate soap, and others donate clothes for children to wear while their clothes are being cleaned. Some schools organize clothing exchanges, particularly for winter wear. A parent coordinator who is familiar with the local bureaucracy can help parents find housing, restore electricity, or receive stipends for fuel oil.

Identifying Home Activities That Support Children's Learning

There is widespread agreement that parents can support their children's learning by reading aloud, providing an environment that is rich in print materials, talking to their child about events and experiences, encouraging their child's interests, taking the child to interesting places, and exploiting the wide range of ordinarily occurring home and community activities for their learning potential (cooking; fixing things; shopping; participating in family projects, activities, and conversations; watching television; participating in religious communities or organized after-school activities).

Pamphlets. Pamphlets are available for parents from several sources that address these topics. For example, the federal Office of Educational Research and Improvement has prepared "Help Your Child Learn to Write Well" and "Help Your Child Become a Good Reader" (no dates); the National Institute of Education has produced "Help Your Child Do Better in School" (no date). The National PTA in Chicago has many publications, including, for example: "Math Matters: Kids Are Counting on You" (no date). These publications provide specific recommendations of things parents can do to extend their children's learning. For example, the PTA's "Math Matters" brochure offers this suggestion among many others: "Using a mileage guide, a map, and a magic marker, let a child follow the route you take, and check how far you have gone. Estimate how much further you must go to your destination or to lunch." Also included are ideas for helping children to recognize shapes and patterns, notice objects that are alike and different, sort objects, and use puzzles and games to support problem solving.

The International Reading Association in Newark, Delaware, has pamphlets available in French, Spanish, and English that focus on such topics as summer reading, using the newspaper (or television) to encourage reading, identifying good books, understanding the relationship between learning and eating well, and preparing one's child for taking reading tests.

Books and Services from Organizations. Many organizations offer a rich array of materials, books, and services that families can use at home to extend and enrich their children's learning. For example, the Home and School Institute in Washington, D.C., offers such publications as *In Any Language: Parents Are Teachers, Grades 4–6* (1984) and *Survival Guide for Busy Parents: Help Children Do Well at School While You Do Well on the Job* (1987); the National Association of Partners in Education in Alexandria, Virginia, offers a publication entitled *Your Child Can Be a Super Reader*; the National Community Education Association in Alexandria, Virginia, offers a workshop package on home–school partnership that can be provided on site.

Private publishers also offer many resources to parents. *MegaSkills: How Families Can Help Children Succeed in School and Beyond* (Rich, 1988) has been widely used, perhaps because it is organized according to skills required for achievement in school (e.g., motivation, perseverance, confidence, teamwork) and provides inexpensive and easy to follow suggestions of activities to do at home that support the development of these skills. College Board Publications offers a book titled *Getting into the Equation* (no date) that focuses on parents' role in helping children to develop math skills through high school, and *Parents as Tutors: Minimizing the Homework Hassle* (Vogler & Hutchins, 1988) emphasizes understanding children's approaches to learning and studying as a vehicle for improving achievement. For an excellent summary of national resources (drawn upon in this section), see *Parents-as-Teachers: A Statewide and National Resource Guide*, available from the Massachusetts Department of Education (1990).

Workshops and Seminars at School. As I will explain in Chapter 8, schools often offer workshops for parents to provide them with specific information about how to support their child's learning through toys, television, discussions, and activities (e.g., "Make and Take" workshops; "Helping Your Child with Homework"; "Math Activities to Do with Your Child at Home"; "Love and Discipline").

Schools may also sponsor workshops that encompass several sessions to give family members a range of ideas about how to increase their children's reading or mathematics proficiency. A side benefit of these multiple-session activities is often to extend or resurrect parents' own skills in these areas. Examples of developed programs that include information and resources for workshop leaders as well as materials for parents include *Family Math* (Lawrence Hall of Science, 1979), *Parents as Partners in Reading* (Edwards, 1990), and *Family Reading* (Goldsmith & Handel, 1990). The San Diego City Schools have developed and piloted a Hispanic Parent Literature Program that brings Hispanic parents together once a month to discuss parenting skills. They learn read-aloud strategies, discover how to ask children probing questions about the literature they are reading, and share stories and poems written by their children and themselves.

Reading at Home. Most educators are convinced of the importance of family involvement in children's reading at home. Whether children read to their parents, siblings read to each other, or parents or guardians read to children, there is good evidence that this effort improves children's motivation to read and reading skill (see Epstein, 1991a; Tizard, Schofield, & Hewison, 1982). Therefore, schools often sponsor read-aloud programs, home reading programs, or book-reading contests to encourage children's outside reading.

One urban school (the Ellis School in Roxbury, Massachusetts) developed a "Raise-A-Reader" Program for the early elementary grades (Krasnow, 1990b). Extra books were purchased for children to take home (with special emphasis on high quality literature that focused on African-American and Latino cultures). Parents helped to sew bright red bags for the books, and a "library card" system was established in each classroom. In one class, students could also borrow stuffed animals that were coordinated with the book content (e.g., a long stuffed caterpillar went home with the children's book *The Very Hungry Caterpillar* [Carle, 1970/1989]). This simple program sparked extensive outside reading and much enjoyment among the children and adult family members. At the Columbia Park and Berkshire Schools in Prince George's County, children get a smiling face token for each outside book read. Each child's record of accomplishment is displayed by classroom on a huge chart that decorates the first-floor school corridors.

Cutright's (1989) book *The National PTA Talks to Parents* is another interesting resource. She lists pages of interesting projects and activities adopted by PTAs across the nation to support children's learning. For example:

> The Neptune Beach Elementary PTA in Jacksonville, Florida, created a program called "Reading: The Road to Success." It turned the school hallways into roadways, with "fuel pumps" recording the number of pages the students read. School librarians became travel agents who "booked" passage

to faraway lands. Demand for "fuel"—books—jumped 95 percent during the program. (p. 121)

School–Library Collaboration. Many schools also collaborate with their local libraries to develop and print summer reading lists for children and families. Local libraries often offer (or might be willing to offer) storytelling, special programs, and contests and prizes to encourage summer and school-year reading. Because some families are not familiar with the resources of a library, a field trip from school for children and their parents using public transportation can be a helpful activity.

Helping with Homework and Schoolwork

Homework Issues. Parents at all grade levels frequently feel confused about how they can best assist the school and their child with homework. Confusion often crops up around the nature of assignments (what needs to be done, how, and by what date); the role parents should take in helping (organizer, supporter, doer, proofreader, monitor); what to do if nobody in the home understands the assignment; what to do if the child seems to be anxious, slow, sloppy, or resistant to doing homework.

Teachers can help parents a great deal by clarifying their expectations about homework in workshops, in writing, and/or in grade-level meetings. Some schools have developed hotlines or video programs to help parents and students deal with questions about homework assignments (e.g., see Warner, 1991). Teachers can make parents feel more comfortable about communicating their concerns about homework if they specifically invite parents to call (identifying specific convenient times) or write notes (e.g., on a folder of the students' work that is exchanged weekly).

At the middle-school or high-school level, a frequent concern of youngsters (and parents) is lack of coordination among teachers regarding the quality and quantity of work expected. Several systems are experimenting successfully with team or house systems, where an identified group of teachers work with the same children, meet regularly to discuss common issues, and are available to talk with parents at scheduled times. A less comprehensive, but still useful, solution is for PTAs to sponsor grade-level or school-based discussions so that teachers and parents can exchange concerns and solutions about homework.

As mentioned above, some schools offer workshops or seminars for parents that increase their knowledge and experience with particular subjects. One school, for example, (the King School in Cambridge,

Massachusetts) offered parents Saturday morning workshops in algebra so that they could help their children at home.

Coordinated Home–School Activities. Some schools provide parents with weekly resource materials so that they can understand what the children are learning in school and supplement specific lessons or units with complementary activities at home. Epstein and associates (1992) have developed a program called Teachers Involve Parents in Schoolwork (TIPS) that helps teachers to use or adapt materials for home learning in the areas of math, science, social studies, and art. Collins, Moles, and Cross (1982) review several programs that extend parents' partnership with teachers in supporting children's learning at home. For example, the Parent Partnership program in Philadelphia provides reading and mathematics booklets to parents as well as a Dial-A-Teacher-Assistance project for help with homework in all basic subjects. The San Diego Unified School District offers materials in English and Spanish that cover homework assignments in reading and mathematics through grade 6. Many special education programs involve parents in supplementing or extending their children's learning at home (Turnbull & Turnbull, 1990). The Office of Research in OERI has commissioned a set of workshops for urban educators called *Schools and Families Together: Helping Children Learn More at Home* (1992) to help educators assist parents to strengthen home learning activities (K–6).

Special Issues for Parents of Color

Parents of color, especially if they are poor, often face special challenges in preparing their children to succeed in school. If the culture and values in the home do not replicate the dominant culture in the school, parents face the challenge of trying to educate their children in both the dominant culture and their own. As members of minorities that experience racial discrimination, parents must also work with their children to help them deal with instances of racism and its meaning to them as individuals and as members of a group. As Perry (1992) explains:

What happens when a child faces overt or covert discrimination in school, by being ignored, rendered invisible, not touched or responded to, given a lower grade, or disproportionately blamed for disruptions? How does the child make meaning of and interpret these events? Is the child being discriminated against because of a personal failing? Is the problem located in the child or in the system? And there is the problem of maintaining a balance. What happens if the child puts "too much blame" on the system? How does one keep the child working and believing that effort matters, and yet socialize him or her to correctly interpret instances when it doesn't? (pp. 85–86)

Perry (1990) clarifies that African-American children face the complex task of integrating three identities: as a potentially successful member of mainstream society in America; as a member of a distinct cultural/racial group; and as a member of an oppressed group. Parents of these children then must address the challenge of helping them to negotiate and make sense of these identities.

As Perry (1990) explains, parents must first build children's knowledge of the strengths and contributions of their own culture and help them to identify with and feel proud of their heritage. Second, parents must help children to understand and experience the norms, values, manners, history, and expectations of the culture that is dominant at the school, so that the children can be seen as having the behaviors and attitudes that make them perceived as being "ready to learn." Third, parents have to help their children recognize instances of racism and learn skills of processing and reacting to these incidents so as to allow them to maintain their equilibrium, self-esteem, pride in their heritage, and belief in the possibility of their own success in the mainstream. Benjamin (1992) maintains that "it is sometimes cumbersome to impart this dual message of survival" (p. 164). She quotes from an African-American mother whose teen-ager attends school in a white neighborhood and who is engaged in a struggle to go along (survive), achieve, and maintain self-esteem:

> I am seeing my child as not willing to be accepting of what you have to do to survive. My child is unwilling to bite his tongue, and it is unfortunate that he has to do it. I tell him in the real world, it is a game, and you have to learn how to play. It goes against my grain, and it annoys me that I have to talk like this, but in reality it is true. I would not be a good parent if I didn't tell my son those people he will be dealing with see him as Black first, and I don't want my son to go out there and think he will be equal to them from their perspective. I want him to feel he is better than the element he is dealing with, but he is not a free spirit in America. He should work toward that, but in the interim, he has to survive and learn how to deal with them, but not give up everything. (p. 164)

Cultural and racial differences help to shape the skills and values youngsters bring to the classroom. Recent ethnographic and cross-cultural studies have helped us to understand some of these differences and their implications for classroom learning. For example, McCarty, Wallace, Lynch, and Benally (1991) describe the Navaho view of knowledge not as a linear hierarchy or a set of isolated skills, but as "a spiraling body of integrated concepts, ideas, and information which support and reinforce each other, continuously expanding to higher levels of complexity and abstractness" (p. 51). In Navaho culture, knowledge is meant to be shared for the common good; moreover, it cannot be given to another or passively received. Each of these assumptions about knowledge influences how Navaho children learn best in the classroom. According to McCarty and colleagues, these youngsters excel in a classroom environment that encourages them to test their hypotheses in an active and interactive learning process and builds on familiar cultural-linguistic content.

Japanese parents have learning priorities which contrast to some degree with mainstream American expectations according to Hess and Azuma (1991). These authors explain that while Japanese parents stress skills that promote cooperation and compliance with authority in their youngsters, American mothers stress initiative and assertiveness. In addition, "Japanese children are expected to probe an issue thoroughly, rather than to push quickly for a 'correct answer'" which dominates the American response (p. 5). The authors explain that Japanese children are trained to rely on internalized diligence and receptiveness, while American children's motivation is prompted by rewards and the teacher's management of the learning context.

Siu (1992) reports that

> Chinese parents, whether here or abroad, tend to exercise more control over the members [of the family], be more protective of children, emphasize more obedience to the parents, provide a higher portion of enthusiastic, positive feedback when teaching young children, value grades more than general cognitive achievement in children, . . . hold children to higher standards, and believe more in effort and less in innate ability than their American counterparts. (p. 14)

Puerto Rican families share some of these values. Important values in this culture that affect school functioning include primacy of interpersonal relationships, emphasis on obedience and following rules, respect for authority, reciprocity, unity of family, and interdependence (Hidalgo, 1992).

Perry (1992) identifies teacher expectations that may conflict with dispositions of the African-American child. She says that

> For the African American child, the issue is not simply the amount of cultural capital, but also the fluency in those dispositions that allow the child to be

viewed as teachable, ready to learn: the ability to be reserved, to subordinate emotions and affections to reason, to constrain physical activity, to present a disciplined exterior. What complicates the picture even further is that these modes of behavior all reside in the domain of participation, with the possibility that constraining behavior in these areas could possibly constrain participation and investment in school. (p. 94)

She maintains that

African American culture is not intrinsically problematic. . . . It is problematic, only because of what it represents to white America, and to the extent that it calls forth in the American mind those images that constrain and limit a teacher's and/or a school's ability to hold high expectations, teach, and assess the African American child as capable and ready to learn. (p. 93)

Indeed, each of the varied dispositions brought by youngsters and their parents to school are valued or problematic only to the extent that they coincide or interfere with teachers' abilities to support and teach. History has shown us that there is considerable variability in the degree to which certain groups are seen as having the potential for high achievement. For example, although Chinese-Americans are generally seen as highly successful in schools today, before the repeal of the Exclusion Act in 1943, one in four Chinese-Americans had no formal education, and only half of those over 25 had received some elementary education (Siu, 1992).

Social scientists have often added to the problems of parents from racial and ethnic minorities by attributing their children's lower school achievement to lesser intelligence (Jensen, 1969), deficient child-rearing practices (e.g., Hess & Shipman, 1965), or lack of motivation to achieve. Lightfoot (1978) summarizes this orientation as it has related to African-American families.

Social scientists have questioned the goodness and adequacy of black parents and distorted or diminished their educative role. Throughout the research literature black family life is described in contrast or in opposition to the social, intellectual, and motivational demands of the school. The *dissonance* in patterns of interaction, values, structures, manners, and style is the major preoccupation of scholars. Furthermore, the dissonance is thought to reside in the *willful* neglect by black parents of their child's preparation and accommodation to school life. Two themes emerge: one that emphasizes conflict and distrust between black families and schools and another that places the blame for the conflict on the family. (p. 129; emphasis in original)

Placing blame for the school failure of minority children on their families is inappropriate because this

- Ignores the role of the school in failing to support some children's school success
- Ignores the long histories of denial of access to academic schooling and good jobs experienced by caste-like minorities (e.g., see Anderson, 1988; Hidalgo, 1992; Siu, 1992; Swap & Krasnow, 1992)
- Ignores the potency of the community in supporting or undermining school success
- Fails to note the differentiated patterns of success within and across racial minorities (see Clark, 1983; Ogbu, 1983)
- Denies the degree to which the conditions of school success are associated with "whiteness" (Perry, 1992).

Investigators have probed the generalized assumption of parental deficiency in poor families, families of color, and families with limited English skills. Several studies, for example, focusing on patterns of literacy and resources to support children's development of literacy, have concluded that contrary to expectations, actual studies of these families have revealed high levels of literacy skill and literacy use as well as high support for their children's literacy development (Auerbach, 1989; Chall & Snow, 1982; Heath, 1983; Taylor & Dorsey-Gaines, 1988). Auerbach (1989) insists that instead of blaming children's underachievement on assumptions that these families are "literacy impoverished" (p. 169), we should focus on trying to change the ways that we reach out to these parents. She argues that more useful reaching out would be characterized by developing curriculum that draws from the richness and uniqueness of the community, helping parents to explore their own concerns and advocate for their own expectations by using literacy to address family and community problems, and freeing parents to become more involved with their own and their children's literacy development.

How can educators and families work together to support the achievement of children of color? As we saw in Chapters 3 and 4, one strategy is to offer activities for parents that make the school's expectations and requirements for success explicit and provide clear guidelines for parents in supporting their children's success within the "mainstream." Another strategy is for schools to use the parents as a resource in developing curriculum that integrates multicultural perspectives into their classrooms and the culture of the school. Bringing multiple cultures into the mainstream by incorporating students' literatures, history, art, and cultural sites into the curriculum of the school fosters continuity between home and school for more of the children and enriches the curriculum for all. However, as the studies referenced in this section explain, students' values, attitudes toward schooling, approaches to learning and teaching, and explanations for success and failure may also have historical and current roots in their cultures. Moreover, these cultural differences are difficult to articulate and are often misunderstood or seen as indicators of pupil or family deficiency. The solution is to work to create schools that are authentically multicultural in their recognition and celebration of cultural differences and contributions among students, faculty, and families.

Thus, a third strategy, represented in the Partnership model, is to include parents and community members in pursuing the goal of helping all children to be successful in school. Educators may need support in discovering the pedagogy that will enable that goal to be reached, in reexamining their own often subconscious beliefs about the characteristics that allow a child to be successful, in learning how to confront racism and discrimination, and in bringing faculty of diverse backgrounds into the fabric of the school.

Parents Helping Each Other

Parents may find it useful to meet with other parents from the school or community to discuss ways of helping their children negotiate their several identities. Bringing children to community institutions that celebrate their particular culture/race and provide access to role models is a strategy for building cultural pride and experience that many parents employ.

In some communities, the instigation or ongoing energy to help parents support their children's learning comes from formal or informal parent organizations. For example, several communities are experimenting with setting up neighborhood study groups, where a group of children gather together to work on homework after school under the supervision of a parent. Because after-school arrangements are so complex for many working parents, some parents have also gotten together to arrange study groups for children in a community setting (agency, library, recreation center, school) where other parents are paid or volunteer to supervise.

Parents of color at the King School in Cambridge organized an "Honors-Bound" group for parents so that they could meet together regularly and discuss how they could support their children's skills and motivation to succeed. Parents and community leaders in San Diego worked through the churches to sponsor "Education Sundays" to enhance communication between local educators and parents; six-session parent workshops on ways of supporting children's success at school emerged out of this initial idea. Parents can organize conferences through a school, community agency, or informal support group around topics of concern. Finally, parent organizations at the local, state, and national level can provide resources, linkage, and models that work. For example, the national PTA assembled 23 national organizations to join in a coalition to support family involvement in schools in a conference in April 1992 (Sommerfeld, 1992).

Parents often ask me what they can do if their schools do not support their interest in being involved at school to enhance their children's learning. My recommendation is to ask educators directly what is deterring them from pursuing a more collaborative strategy, and then to try to resolve or answer their concerns.

A second recommendation is for parents to work collaboratively with each other in trying to accomplish a goal. Educators these days are often legitimately concerned about changing policy or practice for a single parent or small group of parents who are advocating a special or unique interest. After all, another small group of parents may be opposed to the change. Thus, several parents who have a common concern or a good idea are more likely to be influential, and their influence will be extended if they have data that indicate that still more parents share their interest or concern.

To illustrate, I visited a school where a group of parents had developed much influence. When I asked them, "What do you do if you really want something to happen?" a parent responded, "If we really want something we scream together. If there is only one mouth, nobody listens. We discuss, problem-solve, talk to the principal, keep after it every day, or nothing will happen. We talk some more, and got five or six parents together to talk to him."

Sometimes educators are reluctant to move away from traditional practice without evidence that a new strategy will be beneficial and successful. Therefore, a third recommendation is for parents who have access to other resources and models to sponsor a workshop that brings in university advocates or practitioners who have been successful in using a Partnership model. Good sources for ideas include the state and National PTA and the community outreach division of the state Department of Education. Alternatively, a team of parents and educators could visit a school whose practices were exciting. Another source of good programs might be a national organization for schools interested in parent and community partnerships called "The League of Schools Reaching Out." A directory of schools and their practices are available from the Center on Families, Communities, Schools, and Children's Learning in Boston.

From my perspective, advocating for change within the context of a trusting, mutually beneficial interaction is the best way to effect lasting, collaborative change. So a fourth recommendation is to identify carefully those educators who are willing to experiment, and then to initiate a small-scale activity that is highly likely to be successful. The active demonstration that a different model of home–school relationships can be very beneficial for children and adults in one's own system can be very persuasive to other educators looking on.

Sometimes political action is a fifth alternative. For example, parents can spearhead a change in the membership of the school committee, running and supporting candidates who favor more collaborative policies. Parents can also volunteer for leadership positions in local parent councils or organizations and support the initiation of activities that are more collaborative. In addition, parents involved in the selection of superintendents or principals can argue that candidates should demonstrate a commitment to parent involvement in schools. (Incidentally, these same recommendations are relevant to educators seeking a more collaborative approach with parents who have been deterred by a lack of interest from others in the system.)

THE COMMUNITY CONNECTION

Although not a focus of this chapter, individuals and organizations in the community can also function as important resources for children's learning. Cultural institutions such as museums or theaters, recreation centers, after-school programs, and enrichment programs can add important dimensions to youngsters' intellectual, social, and physical growth. Summer programs for recreation, acceleration, or leadership development may enrich children's lives.

Volunteers from businesses, local colleges, or secondary schools can participate in school-based tutoring programs. A recent interview on NPR's "Talk of the Nation" indicated that there are now 140,000 school-business partnerships in the country. In addition to volunteers, businesses may also supply equipment, scholarships for special programs, supplementary funding, contest prizes, technical expertise, management training, or sites for display of children's work. Increasingly, businesses are interested in sponsoring innovative approaches to schooling, where they function as partners with educators and parents in designing new structures for adults' and youngsters' learning. Big Sister/Big Brother or other mentor programs in and out of school can provide role models and individually tailored activities for youngsters. Clergy may offer pastoral counseling, meeting sites, and leadership in developing programs for parents or staff. Job training or exposure to a variety of career options may be offered by business or city/district departments.

Sometimes support for children's learning is indirect. For example, coordinated, accessible, and affordable health and human service programs may provide the underpinnings that make learning possible for a child. The expansion of neighborhood and family networks may also be related to parent empowerment and children's growth (e.g., see Cochran, 1987).

Although clearly not a comprehensive list, these suggestions may be a starting point for brainstorming how the community can join with families and schools in supporting children's learning. In Chapter 8, we will return to the theme of community involvement.

SUMMARY

In this chapter, I have reviewed a range of ways that parents and educators can support children's learning at home and in school. A partnership between home and school is an optimal way to enhance children's learning. Not only does the lack of dissonance between home and school increase children's motivation to learn, but parent involvement in the school as tutors, volunteers, curriculum developers, and mentors extends and enriches what the school can accomplish. Moreover, the school's assistance in clarifying how parents can help at home and in offering useful resources and workshops to families also supports student achievement.

The chapter suggested resources and ideas that would support parents in meeting children's basic needs, identifying activities at home that would support children's learning, and helping with homework and schoolwork.

Parents of color confront particular challenges in preparing their children to be successful in school. Not only do they need to prepare their children to be successfully bicultural, but they also need to help children learn to negotiate instances of racism without losing motivation or self-esteem.

The increasing diversity of our population makes it very important for educators to examine their assumptions about minority families, to integrate the rich perspectives of different racial and ethnic groups into the school's culture and curriculum, and to be responsive to the complexity of parents' roles.

Parents can be an important resource for each other. Local, state, and national organizations offer experienced consultants, good ideas, and many materials that can be used by parents to gather information and explore programs that are working elsewhere. Parent–teacher organizations based in schools can provide a bridge to these resources. When schools are not eager to welcome parents as partners, coordinated action by parents may be an important option.

Finally, we looked briefly at the essential contributions of the community in supporting children's learning.

CHAPTER 8

Providing Mutual Support

It is not a unique idea that parents and school personnel should support each other in enhancing children's growth and learning, but it is often not clear what this means in practice. In the most general sense, all of the outreach to parents from schools that I have described thus far offers support to parents in guiding their children's learning. Conversely, the involvement of parents in their children's growth and learning at home and in school is supportive of educators' work to enhance children's learning. Thus, to avoid repetition and narrow the discussion in this chapter, I will emphasize only some of the ways in which parents and schools provide mutual support. The focus will be on those aspects of mutual support that highlight differences among the goals and assumptions of the four models of parent involvement and therefore generate controversy.

Specifically, in describing school support for families, I will concentrate on the school's role in providing education and support to parents and guardians that need *not* yield immediate or direct benefits to children. In describing family support to schools, I will provide a range of examples, including some forms of support that are controversial, such as families as advocates and decision makers.

Finally, I will discuss the importance of including the community as a third component of this collaboration. Families and schools are embedded in their communities. Businesses, cultural institutions, and health and human service agencies can both contribute vital support to parents and schools and be recipients of critical support from them. Yet how schools relate to the community and its resources is also controversial, with some arguing that the school should becomes a nexus of institutions in the community and a broker of multiple services to children and families, and some arguing that the schools should not and cannot take on any further responsibilities. The goal of this chapter is not to resolve these debates but to place them in the context of different models of parent involvement.

SCHOOL SUPPORT FOR PARENTS

Types of Activities That Support Parents

In this section, I will provide a sample of activities that schools might offer to parents to support them in their roles as parents or individuals. (Please note that the term *parents* is used for simplicity, but in most cases activities would also be open to other significant adults in the child's life.) The defining principle for inclusion of activities in this section is that changes in parents' attitudes, strategies, understanding, or feelings about themselves are the primary focus of the activities. It is expected that children will benefit only indirectly from their parents' participation in these activities. In the real world of schools, it is hard to maintain such a clear and exclusive definition of parent support. Many activities (such as a parent outreach program) fulfill several purposes simultaneously (e.g., parent support, connecting parents to the school, enhancing children's learning). But in this section, I will identify activities whose primary focus is to offer parent support in the more restrictive sense defined above, and then discuss the issues that are raised by parent support of this type.

Activities That Enhance Parenting Skills. Schools sometimes offer workshops, seminars, or discussion programs whose goal is to increase parents' understanding of themselves as parents, expand their parenting skills, increase their confidence, and enlarge their network of adult support. For example, in many schools, the school counselor or school psychologist will offer a support group for parents of adolescents; a special educator will offer a seminar for parents of children with handicaps; a kindergarten teacher or primary teaching team will offer one or two programs on particular issues, such as nutrition, television watching, or selecting books and toys for children.

Schools will also sometimes finance programs offered by skilled facilitators who are not school personnel, who have developed their own programs of parent education or who are trained in offering published programs. Examples of the latter include Gordon's (1975) *Parent Effectiveness Training* (PET), Dinkmeyer and McKay's (1976) *Systematic Training for Effective Parenting* (STEP), or Lerman's (1983) *Responsive Parenting Series*. Each program provides parents several sessions with a continuing group; each helps parents to gain insight into common struggles that parents face; and each offers guided practice for parents that enables them to extend their parenting skills.

Activities That Support Parents' Own Educational Needs and Interests. Increasingly, schools in urban settings have been offering programs to parents that enhance the parents' own skills and/or job potential. Inexpensive and conveniently timed courses in English as a Second Language, group tutorials to help parents gain High School Equivalency Certificates, and programs in resume writing and job interviewing may be very attractive to parents who are seeking to become better educated or more gainfully employed themselves (e.g., see Jackson, Davies, Cooper, & Page, 1988).

When parents are asked what kinds of joint activities they might enjoy, some identify courses or programs that would support a special hobby or interest such as computer literacy, sewing, gardening, photography, or basketball. In a school in Boston, a group of parents confided that they had never themselves seen or taken their children to many of Boston's interesting museums, parks, historical sites, and recreational and cultural activities, and they were interested in finding a way to do so together. Consequently, the parent activities coordinator helped to figure out the correct subway stops and negotiate reduced entrance fees for the group, as needed, for weekly field trips during the summer.

Schools need not always provide all the resources for such programs. Sometimes they provide the space, heat, light, and custodial services for activities or courses offered through a town Adult Education or Recreation Department or a community agency or organization. Sometimes programs may be supported through grants provided by school–business partnerships or by local, state, or regional Departments of Education. Community members with expertise in areas of interest to parents may be willing to volunteer to teach courses or run a workshop, or activities might be offered to parents for a fee that would cover the instructor's time and materials.

Seminars for Parents and Educators. Some schools offer seminars or workshops for parents and teachers together. In one school system where I worked, for example, joint seminars explored the roles of parents, teachers, and specialists in helping children cope with divorce, increasing children's motivation and attention, and developing positive approaches to discipline. It was not easy to establish this format. Initially, teachers agreed to have parents join them only if the parents were teachers themselves. However, when the first seminar on divorce turned out to be very positive, teachers were willing (and in fact eager) to participate again in problem-solving groups that included parents. At the end of the year, one teacher summarized her experiences this way:

Almost all of the workshops, courses, etc., were made up of a cross-section of parents, teachers, and in some cases, schools and levels. Communicating and sharing in this way always had positive results, and I enjoyed broadening my perspective. (Swap, 1987, p. 97)

An urban school offered 2 seminars on parent involvement for parents and teachers, led by a faculty member from a local college. Participants were paid a small stipend for participation, and the seminars were held in a neutral site: a function room of a local restaurant. Each participant was asked to read a few articles about different models or programs of parent involvement. The introduction of common readings permitted some distance from the particular issues at the school; while the more informal, collegial format also permitted thoughtful discussion of parents' and teachers' concerns. In the evaluation, participants mentioned appreciating the honesty of the exchange, the suggestions made for solving problems, and the opportunity to understand each other's perspective.

Outreach to Parents in Their Homes. Many schools have developed formal or informal home visiting programs to establish relationships with parents, communicate information, share tips on supporting children's development, and learn more about the families. In Rochester, a home visiting requirement is built into teachers' contracts, and visits may include tips for parents about home learning activities and strategies as well as sharing information about the child. In other cities, parent coordinators regularly reach out to families in their homes, and sometimes a teacher and a principal or social worker will visit a family together to discuss a concern or celebrate a child's progress. Sometimes teachers will make a visit to each child's home before school begins, to establish a relationship with the family, take a picture of the child to post in the classroom, learn about the child's interests and hopes, and answer any questions the family may have (see Love, 1989, for a description of a first-grade teacher's home visiting program in Waynesboro, Pennsylvania).

Because these home visits demonstrate interest in the child and family beyond what is expected, most families are likely to be responsive to a request for a visit. To ensure the success of home visits in strengthening relationships and creating a climate of support, it is important to help families feel that their home or hospitality is not being judged. As one principal explained to teachers who were beginning a home visiting program, "If someone in the family offers you something to eat, be sure to eat it!" In addition, it is important that school personnel avoid embracing a deficit model and instead see themselves as empowering parents and strengthening themselves by increasing communication and trust. A key element is building on the parents' goals and agenda for the visits. (For further information about a parent empowerment approach to home visiting, see Barr & Cochran, 1992; Cochran, 1987; Johnson, 1990.)

Teachers from the George S. Paine Elementary School in Brockton, Massachusetts (an urban, low-income community), implemented a school-wide home visiting program (reported in Greene & Habana-Hafner, 1988). The program was initiated because unpleasant interactions between parents and teachers had led to a lack of trust of school personnel by parents in the community.

Staff members got together with a consultant to define the kind of meeting with parents that would be most beneficial for creating trust. They also wanted to read and discuss information on different home visiting practices. They decided that the focus of the visits would be to "let parents know that the school wanted what was best for the children and that it was there to provide support for learning—not act in an adversarial role toward children or parents" (p. 25). Teachers did not use the visits to discuss children's problems in school.

To permit teachers to visit homes during the school day on a weekly basis, teachers used a team teaching approach, which was facilitated by small class sizes (1:15). Families were contacted concerning the visits through letters, phone calls, and notices brought home by the children. If parents absolutely refused to allow the principal or a teacher into their home, an appointment was made to see the parent in school. By the end of the year, every family in the school had met personally with a teacher or the principal. The authors report three outcomes.

- Parents call the principal on a regular basis whenever there is a school-related problem with their children.
- An atmosphere of learning and trust has been created.
- Changed attitudes are apparent on the part of both parents and teachers. (Greene & Habana-Hafner, 1988, p. 25)

A home visiting program signals a change in the traditional separation between home and school. It can be a very powerful mechanism for reaching out to parents who are not comfortable coming to school. For parents, having a teacher or principal as a guest in their own home creates a different context for a relationship. When parents host educators, expectations and roles change. For example, discrepancies in power become less central; positive relationships between adults are more taken for granted; and conversations tend to be less formal and more trusting.

Less powerful than visits by school personnel but still potentially very effective in providing support to parents who have not been connected to school are home visits by parent support workers. Ideally, parents from the community with a background in counseling, social work, or education and who are warm, generous, and wise people are hired by the school to reach out to parents as liaisons from the school. At the Ellis School in Boston, a parent outreach program was initiated. As I described in a case study of this school, four parent support workers from the neighborhood

> offered parents friendship; support for parenting concerns; information, modeling and feedback about how parents can support their children's learning at school; referral information about (e.g.), finding improved housing, medical care, or summer program information; and greater connection to the school through information about school activities, hints about communicating with teachers, and support for getting more involved at the school. (Swap, 1990c, p. 51)

The parent support workers let parents set the agenda for their meetings. Positive outcomes included many examples of greater skills among the parents in supporting their children's learning, resolution of several crises in finding suitable shelter or acquiring medical treatment, transmission of information to parents about programs and services available to their families as well as the skills needed to interact with bureaucracies to obtain these services, stronger connection of these parents to the school, and many parents who "graduated" from the program but retained their friendship with the outreach workers.

Technology That Facilitates Family Support. Schools are increasingly taking advantage of technology to support parents in obtaining information about the school or adding to their understanding or skills. For example, high schools have developed videotapes of teachers explaining homework assignments for parents' (and students') benefit. Local cable television stations offer many programming options that could benefit parents, such as interviews with school personnel that include a call-in component, educational seminars for families, and interactive courses.

Although certainly not a state-of-the-art advance, the installation of additional telephone lines in a school can facilitate parental support. Call-in times for individual teachers, homework hot lines staffed by parents and/or teachers, and answering machine information (tonight's homework, this week's spelling words, upcoming school events) are strategies in use in many schools across the country. Some schools have invested in electronic mailboxes for teachers so that parents can access a daily message by calling from their home telephones (Bauch, 1989).

Noticing and Celebrating Parents' Contributions to the School. One component of school support for parents is the explicit recognition of the contributions of parents, family members, and guardians. Although this seems an obvious step for school personnel to take, their busy schedules and the need to keep track of these contributions means that recognition is often not given. I have seen recognition extended to parents or other family members through personal notes written by the principal or a teacher, articles about contributions written up in school or class newsletters and local newspapers, celebration lunches, or all of these. Recognition that is specific, accurate, and not perfunctory helps the recipient feel valued and supported, and often renews interest in continuing to contribute.

Goals and Boundaries for Parent Support Activities

Many educators are convinced that schools should not get into the business of providing direct services to parents. From the perspective of the Protective model for parent involvement described earlier, such activities interfere with the fundamental separation of parent and educator roles. A complementary argument is that given the limited availability of time, money, and personnel, providing services to children, not parents, should be the top priority of schools. A third argument that is often passionately made is that educators are already overworked, overcommitted, and underappreciated, and that other institutions exist whose job it is to provide direct services to families. Educators legitimately worry that providing such services would be like opening Pandora's box: A host of new troubles would rush out, and there would be no end to the demands they would face. Schools that operate according to the Protective model would endorse these arguments and view this multiplication of services and extension of roles as inappropriate.

Those who contend that schools should provide direct support to parents or guardians explain that research demonstrates that changing the attitudes and practices of parents influences all the children in the family. Moreover, for parents who are struggling for the survival of their families (those who need jobs, shelter, or medical assistance), programs on family math or how to help children with homework are simply irrelevant. It is clear that families fall through the cracks because services are fragmented into "absurd slivers" and connections between the services and those who need them are often missed (Schorr, 1988). Only when these more basic needs are addressed through direct service or referrals can a more effective partnership for children's learning emerge between home and school, and many believe that the school is a logical nexus for such activity.

What do we see if we look at these arguments through the lens of the Partnership model? The Partnership model is built on norms of adult collaboration, so the notion of educators seeing parents as they are, as individuals with many strengths and needs, is not alien. Activities that are responsive to the needs and interests of the "whole parent" strengthen the partnership because offering programs to parents releases energy as well as absorbs it. Parents who have been supported by the school are likely to reciprocate by participating in and contributing more to the school. Moreover, even though the primary focus of these activities is parents, children frequently are also beneficiaries, thus contributing to the accomplishment of the school's mission. Finally, educators who reach out to parents also benefit: They are likely to feel less isolated from the community, and participating in adult learning activities can extend educators' own learning and result in different and meaningful rewards.

Within a Partnership model, choices of activities are made jointly by parents and educators, with overall goals and the school mission in mind. This means that the activities that are offered are not as multitudinous as Pandora's troubles, but are pared down by parents' and educators' own priorities, yearly goals, and the resources that are on hand or accessible. Pandora's box contained hope as well as troubles. The optimism and energy that are released by partnership can bring realistically within reach at least some programs that offer direct support to parents.

PARENT SUPPORT FOR EDUCATORS

Parent Roles and Activities

Parents support schools and educators in many different ways. In Chapters 3 and 7, we explored parents' roles as teachers and learners; in Chapter 5, we looked briefly at parents interacting with educators in social events as "just people." Highlighted here will be the roles of parents as audience, helpers, advocates, problem-solvers and decision-makers, and celebrators of educators' contributions.

Parents as Audience. Parents (and other family members) contribute to the school by responding to invitations to watch children perform in musical events, dramatic productions, or sports activities. Science or curriculum fairs provide parents with an opportunity to see students' academic projects on display, and graduation and award ceremonies enable parents to participate in the recognition and celebration of their youngsters' achievements. Parental presence provides recognition not only for the children, but also for the educators' work in preparing children for these moments. Knowing that an audience is coming to review or witness one's work adds energy, motivation, and anxiety to the preparation, as well as more meaning to the outcome. The disappointment that youngsters feel when their parents or guardians miss an important event, and the deflation that educators feel when parental attendance at these events is low, underline the importance of the role of parents, guardians, and family members as audience at school events.

Parents as Helpers. Parents help the schools in many ways: as tutors; classroom, office, and library volunteers; enrichment coordinators; classroom coordinators; and fund raisers. Parents sew curtains for auditoriums, prepare items for bake sales, chaperone dances and field trips, make decorations and plan programs for holiday events, plan and build playgrounds, offer companionship and moral support to teachers, install computers, offer after-school seminars to children and adults, run evening book exchanges, photograph and videotape special events, and reach out to parents new to the school. Sometimes parents aid teachers or principals in translating a good idea into reality by collecting information, contacting key people, or obtaining or developing materials.

These are only examples, of course. Educators as well as children are supported when parents make contributions to improving the physical plant of the school, extending and enriching children's education, supporting the efficient running or improvement of the school, and offering specific help to individual teachers, staff, and administrators.

Parents as Advocates. Parents not only advocate within the school for their own children's interests, they can also be very powerful advocates for the initiation of new policies and programs within and outside of the school, working as individuals or as groups to improve public education. In one school where I worked, for example, parents contributed to the development of an alternative program for troubled youngsters by securing support from local businesspeople for the vocational component of the program, drafting the proposal for the school committee, and advocating for the program at the school committee meeting with professionals from the school. Parents also advocated release time for junior-high-school teachers to facilitate the initiation of parent–teacher conferences at this level.

Melissa Cutright (1989), director of communications and programs for the National PTA in Chicago, summarizes some of what that organization has accomplished.

> We have encouraged individual parents to take an active part in their child's education and to work with others in their community to strengthen their local schools. In order to provide all youngsters with high-quality education, we have sought improvements in our schools, spoken out for adequate funding for public education and worked to assure that public funds are used only for public schools.
>
> In addition, the National PTA has played an important part in teaching generations of Americans to be better parents; in establishing child labor laws and the juvenile justice system; in creating a national public health service; and in developing school hot lunch programs, drug and alcohol abuse prevention programs, the field tests of the Salk polio vaccine, AIDS education programs for home and school and other programs. (p. ix)

State and national organizations and associations initiated by parents of children with special needs such as the Association for Retarded Citizens, the National Society for Autistic Children, and the Association for Children with Learning Disabilities have been instrumental in changing local, state, and national policies to prevent the exclusion of children with handicaps from school, and in ensuring the right of handicapped children to a free and appropriate education in every school in this country.

The potential and power of parents acting as advocates for the school in partnership with educators has been significantly underestimated. In many settings, the fear of parents' interference has made school administrators reluctant to share information with parents and has kept schools isolated from a powerful source of support. In a parallel vein, parents sometimes bypass opportunities to confer with educators and instead proclaim their dissatisfactions with schools in public forums. Although both strategies are understandable, they neglect the potential for working in concert to accomplish joint goals.

Parents as Joint Problem-Solvers and Decision-Makers. Parents support schools by participating in solving problems and making decisions. Examples of parents' involvement in this role include

- Communicating to school officials about staff promotions
- Participating in ad hoc committees (for example, to develop a redistricting policy or to select a new superintendent)

- Serving as members of permanent committees such as a School Improvement Council
- Functioning as advisors to administrators of Special Education or Chapter 1 Advisory Boards
- Being a member of a school-based management team.

In each of these situations, parents' presence is needed to add perspective to problems that need to be solved or decisions that need to be made. Guidelines for involving parents in these roles will be explored in Chapter 9.

Parents as Celebrators of Educators' Accomplishments. It means a lot to educators for parents to notice, appreciate, and recognize their efforts in supporting youngsters' learning and development. In some schools, parents prepare a special meal for teachers each year and publicly acknowledge each teacher's special contributions. Thank you letters, occasional articles in the local newspaper that explain a teacher's special program or approach (especially with pictures), a regular education column in the local newspaper that highlights educators' efforts, and an appreciative note to the superintendent about a teacher, with a copy to the teacher, are all examples of ways to convey support to educators as professionals and individuals.

In my experience, teachers value these communications very highly, sharing them with others, saving notes for years, making comments like, "Your note meant a lot. Sometimes you have no idea whether what you are doing is making any difference." Because there are few mechanisms within the structure of the teaching profession for good work to be acknowledged and appreciated, such efforts by parents or other family members seem to be especially valued.

Goals and Boundaries for Parent Support of Educators

When schools operate according to the Protective model or the School-to-Home Transmission model, school personnel may feel uncomfortable about including parents in any roles that may introduce conflict, suggest equal status between educators and parents in making educational decisions, or blur the clear demarcation of parent and educator roles and responsibilities. When parents function as advocates, problem-solvers, decision-makers, or even celebrators (because celebration suggests evaluation), this involvement can be seen as inappropriate and/or threatening. In these settings, when parents participate as committee members, they are often ignored or underutilized, and parental offers of help as advocates are often refused. Schools operating according to the Partnership or Curriculum Enrichment models are more likely to take advantage of the full range of support that parents may offer.

HOME-SCHOOL-COMMUNITY LINKAGES

The Limits of Home-School Partnership

Changing conditions make it difficult for schools to accomplish the goal of successfully educating all children without embracing partnerships with the community as well as parents. Idealized visions of the past offer little guidance for today's complex realities.

One of the current realities in our search for community must be the acknowledgment of the great diversity of family histories and backgrounds in our country, a persistent theme of this book. Another current reality is that families are functioning in greater isolation from one another than was the case in the past. Coleman (1989) contends that there has been a decline in community function. Contributing to this decline, he explains, are parents working at a distance from their communities, both parents working, and the greater rate of geographical mobility.

A third reality, according to Heath and McLaughlin (1987), is the insufficiency of home-school partnerships for meeting children's academic and nonacademic needs. These authors believe that "the problems of educational achievement and academic success demand resources beyond the scope of the schools and of most families." Many families simply cannot provide their children access to athletic, cultural, social, vocational, and service opportunities outside of school that provide "cultural capital" and motivation for academic work. Those authors believe that this reality "requires us to look beyond family and school to get a full view of the primary networks that make up a child's environment. We can then think of the school in a new way, as a nexus of institutions within this environment" (p. 579). They continue:

> The societal responsibility for educating children necessitates a changed governance structure and planning across the traditional boundaries of the public and private sectors. The school becomes the nexus for community, business, and family collaboration that places academic learning within the nurturant ecosystem of athletic, vocational, and service-oriented agencies and institutions dedicated to mental and physical health. No longer would school boards and district offices focus on the school as a separate institution and attempt to meet only parental demands. Instead, district and state personnel would bring together representatives of local community agencies, busi-

nesses, and athletic groups to decide on shared goals and general strategies for providing coordinated partnership efforts to meet these goals. (p. 580)

Community Support for the School

Mindful of increasing need and decreasing resources, many schools have reached out to the businesses and agencies in their communities to supplement and enrich their offerings (see Chapter 7; also Jackson & Cooper, 1989; Jackson, Davies, Cooper, & Page, 1988; Swap, 1990c; Zacchei & Mirman, 1986). Public and mental health institutions are sometimes willing to locate staff in schools, offer educational programs, donate space, or work in collaboration with school personnel to develop multidisciplinary student support teams. School–university collaborations can provide important resources for school improvement, student interns, collaboration in teacher preparation, and mutual stimulation of faculty and school staff (see Levine, 1992; Sirotnik & Goodlad, 1988).

Accepting resources from the community poses the same kinds of obstacles to schools as accepting resources from parents: When schools operate in a Protective mode, barriers to all types of intrusion are high. Conversely, once schools begin to reach out, the benefits of partnership are very quickly apparent; barriers become permeable; and the challenge becomes one of efficiently managing a rich array of opportunities and resources. Kagan (1989) summarizes the trend towards decreasing schools' isolation from their communities.

> As schools embrace a more comprehensive vision of the nature of the child and of their own role in society, the schoolhouse doors swing open ever wider. To meet the comprehensive needs of children, contacts with agencies rendering health, welfare, and social services have become routine. Special education legislation has propelled interagency collaboration to a new level, and the need to meet the before- and after-school child-care needs of children has fostered many connections between schools and communities. Collaboration between university scholars and school personnel have also helped mend town–gown schisms . . . the conventional vision of the schools as isolated entities is outdated. (p. 110)

Schools Brokering Resources for Families

One of the more radical visions of home–school–community partnerships places schools at the center of a community network of services for families. Though not the responsibility of the school to deliver a multitude of services, the school would help parents and youngsters to understand and negotiate the array of available resources. In Schorr's book

Within Our Reach: Breaking the Cycle of Disadvantage (1988), she states that "the possibility that schools could . . . be a base for the provision of a broad range of social services to students and their families deserves considerably more exploration than it has so far received" (p. 280). The most important lessons she learned about programs that were successful in reaching out to families at risk were as follows:

> In short, the programs that succeed in helping the children and families in the shadows are intensive, comprehensive, and flexible. They also share an extra dimension, more difficult to capture: Their climate is created by skilled, committed professionals who establish respectful and trusting relationships and respond to the individual needs of those they serve. The nature of the services, the terms on which they are offered, the relationships with families, the essence of the programs themselves—all take their shape from the needs of those they serve rather than from the precepts, demands, and boundaries set by professionals and bureaucracies. (p. 259)

Because schools are among the least threatening and most trusted community institutions, because they are geographically accessible, because their focus is not on pathology but universal education, and because they are already serving most families with children in their community, they are a logical choice for the brokering role. Obviously, such a role would become possible only if schools were provided with policy directives, training, and resources to support it. Such a role also depends on the ability of schools to recruit parents who would be willing to clarify the needs of the community to the participating institutions.

The debates that are currently raging in this country about the appropriate role of schools as communities within communities and the role of families in schools cannot be settled here. It is my conviction, though, that schools as they have been organized can no longer meet the academic needs of increasing numbers of today's youngsters. The challenges of changing families and declining economic prospects can be met, but only in the context of a shared vision and the collaboration of families, schools, and community institutions to address these challenges. In Chapter 9, we will explore how to develop structures that encourage mutual support and shared decision making.

SUMMARY

In this chapter, we explored ways in which schools support families and families support schools. The particular focus of the section on school support of families was on programs and activities that attempt to change parents' attitudes, behaviors, strategies, understanding, or feelings about themselves, and only indirectly benefit children. Parent education programs, programs that are responsive to parents' interests and needs, joint programs for parents and educators, and parent outreach programs were among the models considered. Such programs are not congruent with the goals and assumptions of the Protective model of parent involvement, but can be explored within a Partnership model.

The range of ways in which parents support schools was highlighted, including parents acting as audience, helpers, advocates, problem-solvers and decision-makers, and celebrators of educators' contributions to children's growth. Several of these roles also provide challenges to the traditional organization and structure of home–school relationships.

Although the mutual support of home–school partnerships can be a powerful factor in children's academic success and adult satisfaction, many contemporary authors argue that even home–school partnership is not sufficiently powerful to meet the challenges to students' academic success that are posed by changing family needs, declining resources for schools, and increasing burdens on public safety, health, and housing. Rather, the combined and focused resources of the entire community are needed to ensure student success, and the school is seen as a natural nexus for the brokering of these resources. The subject of Chapter 9 is how to develop the policies, structures, and strategies in schools that would make the collaboration among schools, families, and community members more efficient and productive in meeting student needs.

CHAPTER 9

Making Joint Decisions

Joint problem solving and decision making by parents and educators is the fourth element of the Partnership model. Joint decision making is incorporated in programs and policy at the local, state, and federal levels. At the local level, for example, the boards of private schools, preschool cooperatives, and collaboratively run alternative schools provide familiar models of shared decision making. Public school systems frequently engage parents' assistance on ad hoc committees to gather information and make recommendations about such things as school closings, holiday policies, or early childhood program options. Some systems involve family and community members in hiring administrators or in curriculum reviews. For example, Utterback and Kalin (1989) reported that parent involvement in program evaluation saved one school system $60,000 and resulted in the initiation of three major program improvements.

States have involved parents in educational policy and programs as members of state boards of education. Parents sit on state advisory boards that monitor federal programs such as special education, bilingual education, or Chapter 1. In addition, individual states have developed initiatives to encourage parent participation in school decisions. For example, until its state budget crisis, Massachusetts provided supplementary funds to schools for school improvement on a per pupil basis, specifying that parents and community representatives work with educators to decide on spending priorities. In 1984, South Carolina established school improvement councils that mandated parent participation. In 1989, the California State Board of Education issued a comprehensive policy that links parent involvement to children's academic learning. The policy provides state leadership and resources to enable districts to implement policies and programs for their own communities. Parent and community participation at the state level was important to the development of this policy, and further involvement of parents on local planning committees in California is expected.

Until very recently, federal policy had been increasingly explicit about the need for family involvement in educational decisions. For example, Chapter 1 programs have always required parent involvement on advisory boards, but the 1988 amendments to the legislation provide resources for comprehensive parent involvement programs to support children's learning. As noted in Chapter 6, special education legislation requires parent participation on state coordinating councils and in the development of Individual Educational Plans for school-age children. The most recent addition to the legislation, Part H of the Education of the Handicapped Act (1986), also specifies that programs for infants and toddlers should focus on family needs and strengths rather than on the child alone and mandates an Individual Family Service Plan as the vehicle for case management.

The competitive FIRST grants offer federal support for local districts and individual schools to discover and implement new possibilities for partnerships among family, school, and community. But according to an analysis by Ooms (1992), the newest national educational reform proposal (America 2000) "does not acknowledge that educators have any responsibility to work with parents once their child is in school" (p. 24). (See Epstein, 1991b, for a fuller discussion of federal, state, district, and school initiatives to support parent involvement in schools.)

What conclusions can we reach about the many efforts to involve parents in joint decision making? Though I risk oversimplification, I would suggest three. First, simply mandating parent participation in activities or programs guarantees neither active participation nor parent influence on child or program outcome. Research cited in Chapter 6 about parent involvement in IEP meetings provides evidence to support this point. So does the review by McLaughlin and Shields (1987) focusing on low-income parents, which suggests that in many cases parent involvement in advisory councils has been pro forma. The authors suggest that administrators are often reluctant to establish meaningful roles for parents, and parents are unwilling to become engaged on the school's terms. The school improvement councils in South Carolina have reported mixed results (Kijai & Norman, 1990). Even though the councils and their functions are mandated by state law, 20–30% of the principals indicated an aversion to even minimal compliance, and 20–45% of the councils are not making recommendations about school improvement as required.

The second conclusion is that some settings have taken full advantage of the opportunities provided by parent involvement in decision making. Whether involvement was initially prompted by mandate, educators' commitment to hearing parents' voices, or persuasion or insistence on the part of parents, such collaborations have resulted in important benefits for children, schools, and communities. McLaughlin and Shields' (1987) review emphasizes that *active* parent advisory councils bring significant educational and political benefits as well as important resources to the school.

Case studies regularly confirm that when educational leaders listen to parents' voices, exciting improvements can occur. Hagstrom's (1992) story about how his school became a "discovery school" is a case in point. Educators, parents, and community members successfully implemented a comprehensive curriculum revision that drew upon a rich array of community resources and transformed how math and science material was taught. The energy for and direction of the reform were initially sparked by a parent's question, "Our kids are naturally explorers when they're on their own at home. Why can't the curriculum make more of that fact?" (p. 25). Many of the studies of student achievement reviewed in Chapter 1 of this volume also describe the initiation of successful school improvement efforts led by joint parent–educator committees. (For example, see Walberg et al., 1980; also see Williams, 1989, for a comprehensive review of parent involvement in urban school reform.)

The third conclusion is that we have accumulated a lot of information about how and why attempts at joint problem solving and decision making can go wrong, information that can be helpful in structuring successful efforts. To reduce the information to a manageable level, I will focus on analysis of a particular experiment in collaborative decision making, school-based management, which is both new and potentially very exciting, and has already been widely implemented.

SCHOOL-BASED MANAGEMENT

In school systems throughout the country, parent and community representation is being sought on school-based management teams. School-based management (SBM) is considered by many to be the critical underpinning for school restructuring and educational reform. Briefly, the argument that supports SBM is as follows:

1. Schools are failing because they are no longer innovative or accountable.
2. The way schools are managed contributes to school failure, since centralized, unwieldy bureaucracies have lost touch with community needs and failed to elicit or respect the wisdom of local educators.
3. Therefore, if the locus of decision making can be shifted from central administration to individual schools, and if decision making occurs in a richly collaborative context, then schools can be expected to be more innovative and more accountable not only

for the quality of instruction to children but for children's academic success.

In its most ambitious form, school-based management teams are responsible for making decisions for school restructuring and improvement that encompass expenditures, curriculum selection, methods of instruction, scheduling, teacher assignments, assessment of students and faculty, and hiring and firing of teachers and administrators. If the decisions that are made represent departures from traditional practice, then teams are expected to negotiate or request waivers from the central administration or school board.

Not all SBM teams include parents and community representatives. However, interest in initiating experiments in school-based management that do include parents and community representatives is widespread. Leadership for including parents on SBM teams has emerged from many sources. Some initiatives have occurred at the state level. For example, Alabama, Minnesota, and Kentucky have launched major school reform initiatives that assign parents pivotal roles in school governance (Ooms, 1992). Some initiatives have originated with teachers' unions. Experiments in Boston and Denver reflect this pattern (Rothman, 1992). In Dade County and New York City, the superintendent has been an important catalyst, while in Chicago, parents and community representatives sparked this reform (O'Connell, 1991).

Because of the national importance of this effort and the potential for deepening home–school partnerships that it represents, this chapter will explore in some depth what we have learned from experiments with SBM teams that include parents and community representatives. I will also suggest the elements that need to be in place for SBM teams to be productive.

The Potential of School-Based Management Teams

There are many definitions of restructuring. Unfortunately, as is often the case in education, the term has lost clarity and is even used as a label for activities that represent minimal tinkering with the status quo. But the definition that I will use in this chapter is a comprehensive one. This concept of restructuring reflects fundamental changes in thinking about the purposes of schooling and the nature of relationships among adults who contribute to children's schooling. This innovation represents a rejection of the factory model of education, in which children are seen as products to be sorted, certified, or discarded; and teachers are seen as relatively interchangeable dispensers of digested knowledge who function at the bottom of a hierarchical framework.

For many reformers, the model that is sought and that school-based management can support is one in which the purpose of schooling is to find ways to help all children to be successful in school. In this conceptualization, an interactive community of learners replaces the factory model. Teachers are seen as leaders in the effort to spark collaboration, experimentation, and inquiry to support school improvement. The principal is seen as a facilitator of interchange. As Tom Sergiovanni expresses it: "The only thing that makes the leader special is that she or he is a better follower: better at articulating the purposes of the community, more passionate about goals, more willing to take time to pursue them" (Brandt, 1992, p. 47). Parents and community members are seen not only as resources to the school but also as clients. Each school is a unique institution whose mission can and should be shaped by community interests and needs and diversity in background.

In restructured schools, traditional physical and psychological boundaries are blurred, as sharing of information between adults in the school building and across systems is encouraged. Teaching is led by inquiry into students' needs and strengths and discovery of the most effective available practices. Evaluation is conducted by educators not only to assess student achievement but to evaluate the success of particular teaching methods for particular learners. A wide range of resources inside and outside the school is tapped to benefit the growth and learning of children, their families, and educators. In short, in successful restructuring, the school becomes an ongoing experiment in democratic education, and the school-based management team becomes the engine of that reform. (For fuller discussions, see Barth, 1991; Carnegie Forum on Education and the Economy, 1986; Elmore & Associates, 1991; Goodlad, 1984; O'Neill, 1990; Schlechty, 1991.)

Analysis of sbm Experiences

Basic Implementation. Reports of experiments with school-based management record both success and failure. The first level of success is simply a successful transition to a new method of governance. Because the traditional culture of schools is and has been such a powerful source of information and expectation, practitioners feel no small sense of accomplishment in learning how to trust a new process and have it work smoothly. Many studies or reports simply focus on this level of success.

For example, Timar (1989) reported on the Dade County experiment with restructuring and school-based management. He explained that "the goal of restructuring school management in Dade County was decentralization" (p. 272). He cites several factors that contributed to the success of this effort: original inspiration from the Citizen's Committee on Education established by the governor, supportive legislation from the state giving greater managerial discretion to principals, encouragement by the superintendent and the union (which had granted all waiver requests to date), and voluntary participation at the school level.

Timar (1989) reports that major decisions regarding the school did in fact shift from the principal to the school councils. These councils included teachers, counselors, parents, and administrators. They were responsible for most of the school's budget, had a large voice in the hiring and firing of teachers and principals, and shaped curriculum design. Timar did not report on student progress but did mention that the school staff saw these governance changes as necessary conditions for improving curricula and the technology of instruction.

He stated that the school councils changed the school's relationship with parents in two ways. First, parents who served on the council had a significant voice regarding the allocation of resources. Second, since parents participated in decision making, the principal was no longer the single arbiter between the school and the community. Moreover, parent concerns were resolved not by the district bureaucracy but by the school council. (For additional resources on successful transition to SBM, see Aronstein, Marlow, & Desilets, 1990; Burns & Howes, 1990; O'Neill, 1990.)

Initial Results. In general, the effects of SBM on student achievement are not yet fully available. David (1989) summarizes the status of most research on school-based management as follows: "There is surprisingly little empirical research on the topic. Searches of education indexes yield numerous references for school-based management, but virtually all are conceptual arguments, how-to guides, and testimonials from practitioners" (p. 45).

There are understandable reasons for the scarcity of empirical data. SBM has been widely implemented only relatively recently, and the transition from idea to implementation takes at least 3 to 5 years. Moreover, it may not be clear which schools should be included in the data pool, since, as mentioned above, restructuring has been defined in different ways, and SBM teams may also construe their goals in various ways. (For example, I would consider the Comer and Levin reforms reported in Chapter 4 as supportive evidence of positive results from SBM.)

As an example of current "research" on SBM, consider this testimonial in the October 1991 newsletter of Boston's Citywide Educational

Coalition ("Mason," 1991). It illustrates the enthusiasm of the school community for SBM. Interviews of educators and parents from the Mason School's 3-year-old SBM council indicated that the council provided "a forum for developing and maintaining a shared mission" (p. 3). Strong leadership, "honoring what others say" (p. 3), and a long-term commitment to an educational plan seemed to be the ingredients fueling enthusiasm among parents and teachers. Specific achievements noted and attributed to SBM were increased enrollment in the school (from 97 to 263), an integration model that eliminated four substantially separate classes, Accelerated School status, and a new after-school program. Although anecdotal, this testimonial, written by and for parents, argues at least for perceived effectiveness by those most intimately concerned. An additional benefit of the testimonial itself is that it helps to maintain the energy and commitment of adults in these schools and to provide hope and a resource to others.

Case studies can also help to suggest characteristic problems and solutions in implementing SBM. It is already clear that evaluating the effects of school-based management experiments *in situ* is difficult to do, since there are so many variables of context and leadership that affect outcomes. Case studies help us to untangle some of these many strands and to look for similar themes that may emerge across sites. Based on an analysis of these case studies, I will suggest several hypotheses about elements that contribute to the success of SBM.

Hypotheses About Critical Elements of Successful SBM Programs. Timar's (1989) look at the Dade County SBM experience suggests an important hypothesis: that widespread support for SBM from all the major sources of power that influence schools (i.e., central administration, the union, the state Department of Education, the legislature, the governor) is crucial for successful implementation and success over time. David (1991) confirms the need for districts and states to change their own ways of doing business if SBM is to succeed, and specifies the kinds of support that schools need: "To sustain and expand this wave of admirable grass roots efforts . . . districts and states must provide an invitation to change, authority and flexibility, access to knowledge, and time" (p. 12).

Further information is needed to establish whether schools can be successful in restructuring only when provided with the unanimous support of all the power sources, as in Dade County; or whether success may result with particular combinations of support, but not others. Finally, it is crucial to determine how schools or communities could mobilize such support if it does not exist.

Another theme that emerges from case studies and other research is that the principal plays a key role in the success of SBM. The principal needs to feel comfortable in a facilitative, collaborative role, or be willing to engage in training that would generate the alternative leadership skills required. Based on my conversations with other consultants and researchers and my own direct experiences with school-based management efforts, this fact emerges very clearly. If a principal is inept in structuring active, focused, intellectually exciting, and collaborative meetings; refuses to share authority or leadership; punishes individuals who disagree with him or her; and will not seek or use help to gain facilitative skills, SBM has little hope.

An exploration of the failure of site-based governance in Salt Lake City illustrates this point. Malen and Ogawa (1988) found it "confounding" that these Utah councils, though provided with "broad jurisdiction, formal policy making authority, parity protections, and training provisions" (p. 251), did not create a context in which teachers or parents could wield influence in significant decisions. They found that "the principals were inclined to preserve, not alter, traditional authority relationships . . . and were prone to protect the decision-making authority traditionally vested in the role of principal, [and] to minimize participation in areas traditionally designated as 'administrative turf'" (pp. 260–261). According to the authors, the principals' orientation was reinforced by the selection of cooperative participants, norms of propriety, a stable environment, control of council processes, and an absence of district intervention when sites did not follow prescribed policies.

Although parents should have felt empowered, they felt constrained by several factors: being invited to join rather than being elected by a constituency, having ambiguous guidelines, participating in meetings where agendas were noncontroversial and established without their participation, and feeling uninformed about school activities and operations. Although they had received some district training, were well educated, and had issues to bring to the table, they did not know how to use the council to air their concerns. The authors indicated that the "interview transcripts are replete with parent and teacher requests for additional training" (p. 267).

To shift from concepts and research to practice, what is to be done if active support of the principal is necessary for SBM, but the principal is not interested in this approach or is unsuccessful in developing the required skills? Understanding possible reasons for resistance is a first step. There are good reasons to expect significant opposition to SBM from many principals. For example, the shift from a hierarchical to a collaborative management style is a major one, and many principals, particularly in urban settings, have chosen to be principals and have been rewarded over time precisely because of their effectiveness in exercising decisive authority. There is always legitimate doubt among experienced educators that any educational reform will last more than a few years, which is certainly a reason for delaying a commitment to changing oneself or the school. Moreover, there continues to be support for the authoritarian principal in popular culture: For example, a recent feature film celebrated an urban high school principal who used a bullhorn to establish order and responded with contempt to parent and teacher concerns. There are additional reasons for opposition: Restructuring is difficult, time-consuming, and demanding as well as rewarding; some are not ready to make this kind of investment. Finally, though interested, some principals believe that their schools are not ready for SBM and first need to take some preliminary steps that build trust and order.

If other educators and community members believe, in contrast, that SBM is a good fit for the school, and the principal remains unwilling to negotiate, there are some options. Those with responsibility for offering administrative training and evaluating the principal may offer a combination of incentives and support for exploring SBM, as well as disincentives for nonparticipation. Incentives may include, for example, substantial grants to schools that volunteer to participate (a strategy used in New York City), compensating principals to participate in national training institutes, or support for school-based consultants to develop leadership in the school on an ongoing basis. (It is not necessary that the principal be the chair of an SBM council, and some very successful efforts in SBM have involved the principal in an active support role.)

Disincentives can include negative evaluations from school councils or superintendents and pressure from professional organizations, colleagues, teachers, and parents. Sometimes principals can actually be removed from their position by school councils (as has occurred in Chicago) or be transferred to a community where their skills match community interests. In most communities, SBM has been undertaken as a voluntary effort, and observation of success in sister schools that have committed to this reform might spark re-evaluation and experimentation. When substantial numbers of teachers and children request transfers to other schools, such a groundswell may offer another kind of incentive for exploration.

In the long run, the persistence, importance, and success of restructuring will offer the most persuasive reasons for principal involvement. It is these results that will transform the cultural context that defines the characteristics of successful administrators and the programs of institutions that prepare them.

Another hypothesis worth testing is that a necessary condition of successful SBM is training for all participants, both initially and as the group matures or adds members. According to Jennings (1989), this training should include sharing information about the administration, curriculum, and organization of the school and the purpose and rules of the council. Training should also help participants to articulate the principles of team building and to practice them in simulations, especially the complexities of disagreeing and reaching consensus. I would also suggest that training focus on helping participants to understand and articulate the transformation of values and philosophy about schooling that SBM represents. This goal is important because the training of the participants on an SBM team is an important step in educating their constituencies and eventually the whole community about the potential of restructuring.

A case study provided by two educators in Winona, Minnesota, offers another useful hypothesis. Sambs and Schenkat (1990) describe trying to understand why their "innovative efforts in site-based management and state-of-the-art projects and . . . use of a vision statement—all the right pieces—were not jelling" (p. 72). Their conclusion: the need to find a purpose to drive their efforts. They found this purpose in two statements: All students can succeed; and schools control the conditions of success. These statements led the planning committee (including parents) toward purposeful, systematic, and integrated efforts to change school "beliefs, conditions, practices, and traditions" (p. 75).

My experience with several schools supports these authors' hypothesis that a strong sense of purpose related to children's success is necessary to fuel fundamental restructuring over time. However, in many schools, the first efforts of the council are very practical and focus on changing the conditions of teaching for teachers: creating more equitable schedules, smaller class sizes, more control of curriculum, access to professionally useful knowledge. Such changes in policy and practice may be essential for teachers to trust that their voices and experiences will have effect. Similarly, a focus on particular program or equipment needs may dominate parents' initial goals. One parent explained to me that her enthusiasm for SBM began when she requested that the school fix broken street lights on school property, and this goal was actually realized.

Yet council time can be completely occupied with complaints or debates about school uniforms, after-school programs, or cafeteria food. The problem is that resolving these issues, though important, may be seen in the community as self-serving, and the council may come to be viewed as a vehicle for providing more power to particular constituencies in a closed network. Moreover, restructuring and SBM may have no long-term effect on student learning. Unless the efforts at restructuring are driven by an integrative purpose that forms the framework for radically improved teaching and learning to benefit all children and the community as a whole, the transforming, energizing, and moral potential of restructuring will not be realized.

CONCERNS ABOUT JOINT DECISION MAKING

Partnership between parents and educators is not appropriate for all schools or all cultures. As mentioned in Chapter 4, when there is consensus between families and educators about what the role of each should be, when children are succeeding in school, and when the community is homogeneous, the need for regular contact, joint decision making, and the creation of mechanisms to negotiate differences is minimal.

When these conditions are not in place, educators and parents may still be reluctant to experiment with the solutions of restructuring or partnership, in part because of the barriers identified in Chapter 2. In my experience, it is *particularly* the issue of joint decision making that causes educators and parents to question their commitment to partnership. Parents, caretakers, and other family members worry that agreeing to participate on a committee or council will be a waste of time. Some parents explain that their time and opinions are not respected or influential: They are there just for show. Other parents feel that there is just too much distance in language, education, class, race, or culture for them to feel comfortable at the school. Others believe that the school should just get on with it and accept the responsibility for what happens in the school. From my perspective, it is the school's responsibility to make parents or other caretakers feel important, useful, respected, and needed. Until these conditions are met, parents are quite appropriately skeptical.

Educators also have legitimate reasons for being unenthusiastic about sharing decision making with parents or caretakers. As voiced by teachers, those concerns that I have found most central, inhibiting, and actually derailing are

- Parents may not recognize my expertise and training. Why should parents have an equal voice in curriculum decisions? I've had many years of training to prepare me for what I do. Why is teachers' expertise given so little respect? Do patients have an equal voice with physicians in deciding on their medical treatment?

- Parents will advocate for the particular needs of their individual children, not for the needs of all the children, let alone for the teachers or principal. This babble of voices and needs will create chaos. (And, by the way, some parents can be very cruel in the ways they talk to us and about us when they disagree with what we are doing.)
- Parents' contributions to educational decisions may be influenced not by academic arguments but by religious or political beliefs. The school cannot be an arena for evangelizing or politicking. We teachers must not permit censorship or control of what and how we teach.
- The parents that usually get involved in decision making represent only one subgroup of the school. Why should these activists be given more power than other parents?

These concerns cannot be dismissed, and each will be considered in turn. In addition, I want to present a more careful definition of what partnership means relative to decision making and a more explicit delineation of the conditions that make partnership possible.

Disregard of Teacher Expertise

Partnership in decision making does not assume that parents or educators have expertise in the same areas. Partnership entails recognizing each other's legitimate authority. The task is to create a context in which the important information available to parents and educators (and others outside the community) can be usefully exchanged in order to make decisions that affect children, educators, and the larger community. In the example above, teachers *do* know most about curriculum—and parents know most about the interests and strengths of their children. What is generally missing in our schools is an exchange: one in which teachers can use parents' knowledge to help them select among curricular options or develop further options; and parents can use teachers' knowledge to help them understand the goals, benefits, and limitations of different curricular approaches. If the goal is to help all children succeed, then both kinds of information are critical, and collaboration is more effective than domination in making useful selections.

To continue with the medical analogy, perhaps the best doctor-patient relationship is also a partnership, in that the most appropriate treatment is dependent on complete and accurate exchange of information, and the client should decide among treatment options based on an understanding of goals, benefits, and disadvantages. Some parents and some patients, some teachers and some physicians are happier with an authoritarian approach: Perhaps this is where choice within districts should be available to all.

Advocacy of Individual Needs

In order for parents to make well-considered decisions, they must be informed. Particularly for parents participating in school-based management who will be sharing responsibility for the council's decisions, the need for information is critical. In a larger context, in order for parents or caretakers to respect the culture of the school and the needs of the school's many constituents, they need to learn about them. Part of the work of a council, therefore, is to identify members' information needs; to share documents; and to create forums, activities, and exercises that will respond to members' questions or need for information. Being the recipient of this kind of information and responsibility almost inevitably extends "ownership" beyond one's own family. Having one's own concerns listened to, respected, and acted on can also build ownership and trust.

Influence of Religious or Political Beliefs

There is no question that a significant barrier to partnership is erected when parents (or sometimes faculty) attempt to shape academic choices based on religious or political beliefs. Fundamentalist objections to certain literature, approaches to sex education, or evolution are familiar examples; parental insistence on exclusively Afro-centric or non-Western curriculum is a more recent example. Often such arguments are drawn from a complex network of intricately interlocking values and beliefs, such that those who do not agree with the individual's point of view are seen as morally bankrupt as well as wrong. Often these beliefs arouse opposing convictions as well as strong feelings in the listener. Often both sides feel they have the only truth; thus, opportunities for respectful listening and compromise are not available. Concern about protecting the rights of those who hold minority views complicates this picture still further.

Three suggestions are offered, admittedly incomplete. Assuming that the confrontation is occurring in a group meeting, the first suggestion is to listen carefully to the concern, while not permitting serious derailing of the agenda. If the scope of the meeting does not permit time for resolution, the importance of the issue can be acknowledged, and a committee named to study the controversy and report back within a specific time frame. This committee's time should be structured to include the exchange of information, including research or outcome data if relevant and available, and the exploration of possibilities of negotiated compromise. A second suggestion is to create a pilot project to test out alternatives or to provide parents or faculty with some options, if appropriate. A third is to include in the council's bylaws very strong guidelines related to attacks on individuals (that is, that problems, not people, should be attacked), and to enforce the guidelines.

There are times when it is very easy to recognize that a viewpoint is clearly wrong, illegal, or impractical, and educators should certainly say so. Rejecting a parent's position without being patronizing or disrespectful is a useful skill. (The same guidance applies to parents who feel they must reject an educator's view.) But usually the issues are complex, and individuals' judgment can be seen as relative. Our democratic society has courts to maintain the balance between the rights of minorities and the will of the majority: Democratic schools have not developed an equivalent structure, though courts continue to be a final resort.

Unequal Representation of Parent Subgroups

Educators are quite right that parent involvement on an SBM council or other important decision-making body should not be confined to a particular subgroup in the school (most commonly, officers in the PTA; white, middle-class parents; African-American or Latino parents when their children constitute a majority in the school). The council *should* represent all major constituencies. The solution to this problem is not to abandon joint decision making, but to prevent (or remedy) limited access. Council bylaws must mandate representation; selection processes must ensure them; and outreach of the kinds noted in Chapter 5 must seek out and prepare representatives from all constituencies for leadership roles inside and outside of the school. (Incidentally, the same issues arise for staff and can be dealt with in the same way.)

SUGGESTIONS FOR JOINT DECISION MAKING IN SBM COUNCILS

Providing comprehensive guidelines about how to initiate or improve SBM councils is beyond the scope of this review. However, to conclude this chapter, a list of resources is offered, as well as some suggestions of particular relevance to the use of SBM councils as vehicles for home-school partnership and joint decision making.

Resources

School-based management has received a lot of attention, and sources of help include

- State education agencies (note especially California's Parenting and Community Education Office)
- National parent advocacy groups (note the National Committee for Citizens in Education in Columbia, Maryland)
- Federally supported programs (such as the Southwest Educational Development Laboratory, the Technical Assistance to Parent Projects in Boston, the ERIC Clearinghouse on Educational Management in Eugene, Oregon)
- University connected institutes and consultants (for example, Boston University's Boston Leadership Academy; the University of Oregon's Center for Educational Policy and Management)
- How-to guidebooks (e.g., Bailey, 1991; Marburger, 1985; Murphy, 1992).

Recruitment, Selection, and Retention of Parents

Recruitment. The best way to develop a large pool of interested parents or caretakers for a council is to establish a rich and varied network of family involvement activities, at least some of which appeal to all families, as outlined in Chapter 5. Family involvement with the school and school personnel in school, at home, or in the community creates a network of relationships and an understanding of the culture of the school that is extremely useful for attracting and preparing parents to be council members. However, when parents from necessary subgroups are not represented, schools have reached out through

- Identifying an active representative of that subgroup (parent, community member) who is willing to recruit others
- Inviting possible candidates who might be concerned about making a long-term commitment to test their interest by joining ad hoc problem-solving groups that require a more limited commitment
- Inviting potential recruits to be guests at council meetings to give them firsthand knowledge of the group, and/or appointing poten-

tial future members of the council to be substitutes or to serve a
more limited term
- Scheduling at least some of the meetings at times and places that
  are convenient for the parent and community members and offering child care if needed.

Selection. Parent representatives can be appointed from a list of
volunteers by the principal, the SBM chair(s), and/or the school's parent
association; elected by the parent body; or chosen by some combination
of these strategies.

As mentioned above, there is an understandable tendency for those
in leadership positions to want to work in a comfortable group and
preserve the status quo. Nonetheless, it is important for the long-range
success of the council that it be truly representative of the parent community. Thus, the goal is to assemble a group of parents who are from
different economic and ethnic backgrounds, who represent different
points of view and are willing to articulate them, and whose children are
at different grade levels. The selection process adopted by the community should reflect those aims. If parent membership on the council is
initially nonrepresentative or becomes so, then the council itself, the
chair(s), or a council subcommittee, perhaps aided by an outside consultant, could help to pursue the solutions that pertain in the specific setting.

It is sometimes useful to recruit at least one parent who has been
outspokenly critical of some aspect of school policy, not only because of
the symbolic value of such an appointment to the community, but also
because of the energy such an individual often can bring to the group.
Moreover, membership in the group provides opportunities for the individual to learn more about the multiple constituencies and needs the
school must negotiate.

Marburger (1985) suggests that a council range in size from 9 to 23
and that there be parity in numbers between representatives of the school
(administrators, teachers, specialists) and representatives of the community (parents, community members, students at the secondary level).
Parity in numbers does help parents feel free enough to express points of
view, especially divergent ones, and a fairly large group creates more
opportunities for mutual support and continuity when some members are
(inevitably) unable to attend.

Retention. Sometimes a group that begins as representative becomes increasingly unrepresentative over time. The problem may be
difficult to isolate and work on if attendance is not taken or excuses for
nonattendance seem quite reasonable. The most common reasons for

diminished attendance are that individuals do not find the work important enough to make the sacrifice of time that is required; the meetings are boring, inconclusive, or inefficient; and/or individuals do not feel valued, listened to, or respected for their contributions.

For parents who do not have experience with committee functioning, sensitive efforts to draw them out may be required, such as small group brainstorming sessions, asking each member for an opinion on a particular topic, reporting out to a large group without identifying the contributions of individuals, and so on. As an example of a successful intervention, one parent who had been very shy as a council participant told me proudly that the principal (chair) of the council said that the group could not make a decision on a certain topic until each of the parents had been heard from. This explicit invitation was necessary for her to feel welcomed into the group.

There is also a need for awareness that standards for social interaction and ways of communicating respect may vary among individuals from different cultures. As suggested in Chapter 6, differences in understanding generated by unspoken rules about eye contact, interrupting, length and meaning of silences, comfortable physical distances, the significance of arguments, or male/female expectations may cause discomfort or even alienation. If different interpretations of nonverbal signals or social expectations seem to be interfering with the work of the council, then bringing in a professional consultant or valued member of the community to help the group discuss these issues would be important.

Training: Formats, Content, and Intensity

I have been impressed with the fact that effective councils maintain a continuous investment in training. Many of the experiments in SBM already cited document extensive investment in training council members. For example, in Prince George's County, Maryland, two members of the central administration staff are available to consult with administrators and councils to support the Comer process; there are yearly retreats; and schools send teams to the Yale Child Study Center for several days in the summer. In California, when the Accelerated Schools program was getting started, graduate students from Stanford who were experienced principals were available to work with the pilot schools on a weekly basis. Now schools that are interested in becoming Accelerated Schools must participate in summer institutes and extensive follow-up training. When the Schools Reaching Out project (Swap, 1990c) initiated school-based management in participating schools in Boston and New York City, it became clear that consultants were needed to model how to lead and participate fully in a democratic council. Council members had to learn to challenge authority, express opinions openly, negotiate differences, compromise, and support the efficient use of time. In one school, a consultant was identified who provided support, concrete information, and feedback to the principal (chair). This support helped the principal organize and lead meetings in ways that encouraged participation.

Because restructuring demands changes in traditional values, attitudes, behaviors, structures, and roles, training and consultation are essential. Resources are available through professional organizations, training programs for particular reform models, universities, and private consulting firms. When identifying a consultant, it is important to select individuals with experience in schools and SBM teams, an orientation to continuous learning, curiosity about the unique challenges of the site, deep respect for educators and parents, and flexibility in approach. Note that the group is likely to have varied needs as it evolves and might require consultants with different strengths at different points in its history.

My experience has illuminated the willingness of parents and educators to explore the challenges of restructuring. Long-term commitment is possible when constituents can be assured of support in taking risks, when help is provided at key points, and when benefits to children, themselves, and the community become apparent.

SUMMARY

This chapter has explored options for joint decision making between parents and educators. Perhaps the most challenging of the four components of partnership, collaboration in decision making raises important questions about home–school boundaries.

Beginning with a brief overview of federal, state, and local experiments with joint decision making, we concluded that mandates for collaboration are not sufficient for success. Nonetheless, there are many examples of collaborations that have proved beneficial for youngsters' achievement and adult satisfaction.

The focus of the chapter was school-based management, a vehicle for the radical restructuring of schooling and home–school connections. We examined the potential of SBM and reviewed the successes and failures of many experiments across the nation in order to develop hypotheses about what makes SBM councils work.

Finally, we looked at several familiar arguments against involving parents in school-based decision making, offered responses to those arguments, and suggested strategies that encourage joint decision making by parents and educators on SBM councils.

CHAPTER 10

Three Paths to Partnership

And should I then presume?
And how should I begin?

T. S. Eliot, "The Love Song of J. Alfred Prufrock"

Rhetoric and reality are far apart when one evaluates the status of home-school partnerships in this country. National, state, and local leaders repeatedly emphasize the importance of home–school collaboration. But what is the reality? Evidence cited in Chapter 2 indicates that relatively few parents are actively involved in schools. It also appears that relatively few schools have made significant efforts to reach out to parents in nontraditional ways. It is difficult to be precise in this conclusion because we have not invested in the kinds of research that would allow us to evaluate accurately the current status and results of home–school involvement programs. As Joyce Epstein (1991b) explains, "There are still vast gaps in our knowledge that can only be filled by rigorous research and evaluation of particular types of school/family connections in support of children's learning" (p. 349).

Policy directives and professional preparation institutions offer little guidance to interested educators and parents who would pursue collaborative efforts on behalf of children. As mentioned in Chapter 9, federal policy, as reflected in America 2000, does not offer guidelines or support for strengthening family–school partnerships. Concerned about this lapse, a flyer from the National PTA states: "Despite the rhetoric and speeches by policy makers about the importance of parent involvement, the goals bypass parents almost exclusively" (quoted in Ooms, 1992, pp. 24-25). Administrators struggle with the absence of coherent policy. Based on a national study of 42 urban schools identified because of their interest in reaching out to parents, Davies, Burch, and Johnson (1992) concluded: "Our most important observation and conclusion is that all of the schools studied are engaged in substantial reaching out activity

---

I am indebted to Joyce Epstein for the phrase "paths to partnership" used in the title of this chapter.

without the benefit of a clear, comprehensive, and supportive policy system" (p. 142). As a principal explained in an interview, "I feel like I'm in an ocean of rules and programs without any maps" (p. 121).

Some other countries do much better. In Strathclyde, Scotland, for example, the largest educational area in the United Kingdom, a written policy forms the framework for community-based integrated programs of services for young children that are organized through the Department of Education. The 10-point policy provides for joint planning and implementation of the services by parents and staff and partnership with voluntary organizations and community groups providing these services throughout the region (Strathclyde Regional Council, 1990).

Despite the rhetoric that teachers must be leaders in reaching out to parents, Davies, Burch, and Johnson (1992) found that teachers in their sample of schools "reaching out" were not doing so: "With some exceptions, teachers are not reported to be the primary initiators of family and community partnership activities" (p. 133).

This reality is not surprising. Our teacher preparation institutions are doing very little to prepare future teachers to collaborate with parents. A recent survey reported that 70% of first-year teachers felt that parents were their adversaries (Ooms, 1992). Teacher preparation programs continue to give minimal attention to the development of skills and strategies that would change these prevailing negative attitudes. According to a recent survey of 505 randomly sampled teacher preparation programs (Brown, 1991), although 94% of the respondents agreed that "preservice teachers need to be educated in effective home–school communication techniques," fewer than 6% of the colleges had a course on parent–teacher conferencing (p. 9). Of those responding that such content was offered as *part* of a course, 81% explained that it constituted only 1–10% of the course. To my knowledge, very few teacher preparation programs require even a single course related to parent involvement. An ominous warning for the long-term status of this topic in teacher preparation programs is the fact that the 1990 standards of the National Council for Accreditation of Teacher Education do not even mention parents, families, or communities (Ooms, 1992).

For those interested in initiating partnerships, obstacles such as those described above may seem overwhelming. Because my experience suggests that partnerships *are* possible, the remainder of this chapter is designed to encourage images of possibility and to share strategies about ways of beginning. Though not a comprehensive guide, this review also suggests ways of averting problems that are frequently encountered.

I address my remarks primarily to educators. Although parent and community advocacy groups have been vital forces in initiating dialogue and programs in some communities and this information is relevant to community activists, the primary responsibility for reaching out belongs to educators. Recognizing that individuals and schools will be at different stages of readiness to reach out, three different paths to partnership are described that require increasing levels of commitment: from focused, circumscribed efforts, to comprehensive programs, to restructured schools. Each of the three paths can embody the principles of partnership outlined in this book: two-way communication, mutual support, enhancing children's learning, and joint decision making.

PATH 1. ESTABLISHING A LIMITED PARTNERSHIP FOR CHILDREN'S LEARNING

Program Options

When resources, time, or support are limited, but one or more educators wishes to reach out to families to support children's learning, there are many productive options. For example, a teacher in a Georgia school was instrumental in initiating school-day workshops for parents of first-grade students. The goals of the workshops were to help families understand the aims of the curriculum, gain firsthand experience with materials, and extend their children's learning at home. Children's hand-made invitations encouraged parent involvement; a schedule that allowed some teachers to be with the parents while others taught the children provided needed flexibility; and arranging for parents to stay for lunch after the workshop created time for informal sharing. The idea worked so well that six workshops are now offered to parents during the year by the first-grade team, and teachers from the other grades are developing their own workshops. A network of parent volunteers was an unanticipated benefit of the workshops (Joan Howard, personal communication, March 21, 1992).

As another example, two parents who were educational aides in the Miles Park School in Cleveland initiated a 6-week summer enrichment program. The principal and teachers assisted in developing the curriculum. Focused on reading skills, field trips, and other enrichment activities, this program led to improved behavior and higher reading scores among the 62 children (Davies, Burch, & Johnson, 1992).

A colleague in Boston had an idea for initiating a dialogue with parents about their children's reading achievement. Teachers sent each family a tape of their child reading aloud in school. The only instruction was, "Please let us know what you think." Over 90% of the families responded by telephone or letter, in English, Spanish, and other languages. So many parents came to school that extra staff had to be assigned to listen to families' reactions (John Cawthorne, personal communication, February 13, 1992).

Key Elements in the Examples

Each of these examples focuses on children's learning, especially reading achievement. Each promotes two-way communication between families and teachers in assessing children's achievement and contributing to improving it. In each case, the ideas were developed at the local school level with the active support of the principal. In each case, though the initial outreach was limited in scope, positive outcomes led to further collaboration among educators and parents.

Suggestions for Creating a Limited Partnership

Set Priorities. If minimal resources demand that one choose among possible programs, my first priority would be activities that focus on enhancing children's learning. This might mean offering a workshop on selecting good books for children, initiating a dialogue with parents about ways to support children's learning at home, or inviting parents to help with an oral history project inside or outside the classroom. I would suggest this focus in preference to such activities as parent support groups or field trips unrelated to the curriculum in order to avoid fragmentation of effort, highlight the utility of parent involvement, and maximize the likelihood of seeing positive effects on student achievement.

Build Participation. Persistence and persuasion may be needed in the beginning to demonstrate that the family's involvement is vital to support children's learning and that all parents will be welcomed and respected. Children's invitations, newsletters sent home, personal invitations from the teacher, a telephone chain, or a combination of these strategies may be useful at first to underline the teacher's (or school's) commitment to partnership. If these elements are in place, and parents are convinced that educators believe that their involvement is important and will help their children, participation generally builds very quickly.

Establish Two-Way Communication. Establishing two-way communication is essential. One-way programs (for example, those that exhort parents to improve their deficient parenting skills) are not likely to attract returning crowds. In general, opportunities to exchange information and support are more rewarding and empowering for parents than simply being recipients of educators' expertise. As explained in Chapter 5, two-way communication builds stronger relationships over time and contributes to a community of learners. However, if there has been a long history of distrust between parents and educators, or families' cultural backgrounds lead to expectations that educators should be authoritative, then it may take longer to achieve open exchange of information. Checking with parents about their reactions to programs and discovering the expectations families from diverse backgrounds have about school can be critical to the long-term success of an outreach effort. It is often true that parents who come from a culture that does not value parent involvement in schools will nonetheless be willing to participate actively if they learn that their involvement will contribute to their children's success in this setting (see Siu, 1992).

Draw on Local Expertise. When initiating limited partnerships for student learning, it makes sense to use local expertise and easily available community resources. For example, a local college or museum may have curriculum materials that educators could review, borrow, or adapt; a library of educational videos that could be tapped to add interest to a workshop; or staff who could co-teach a seminar.

Acknowledge Success. It is important to acknowledge and celebrate activities that support partnerships, regardless of their scope. Small-scale efforts that are successful are useful starting points for further outreach because they build the confidence of organizers, whet participants' appetites for more, and often draw in others who are willing to contribute to subsequent efforts. Rather than wondering where all the others are, those who come should be acknowledged as valued pioneers.

Ally with Principals. Principals play a crucial role in initiating outreach activities. They can model partnership through their own activities and attitudes, set policy that encourages outreach, provide resources and support for activities, facilitate when barriers are encountered, and reward risk-taking. Principals also need to be aware of the potential for burnout of committed parents or educators who inadvertently become responsible for maintaining a good program over an extended period. To reduce this risk and to promote institutionalization of the concept apart from the individuals who began it, principals can privately and publicly recognize and celebrate these efforts, find funding or other incentives to compensate key staff, and seek additional program organizers so that responsibility can be shared or rotated.

When principals are not encouraging or at least permissive, initiating outreach is much more difficult. In this situation, teachers' efforts tend to be confined to families of children in their classrooms. The satisfactions that emerge from improved connections to families, though sustaining, are not easily shared with professional colleagues or expanded into school-wide programs. Principals who are not initially supportive of family outreach may become so over time through professional training, support or pressure from central administration or parents and teachers within the school, and/or exposure to the positive effects of successful programs.

PATH 2. BUILDING A COMPREHENSIVE PROGRAM: NETWORKS OF MUTUAL SUPPORT

Program Options

A comprehensive program is one that reaches out to children and families in multiple ways by offering a variety of school and community program options that appeal to diverse families. The Martin Luther King Middle School in Boston, for example, offers several programs in each of six different areas, as listed below (an example is provided to illustrate each area).

1. School help for families (a staffed parent center)
2. School–home communication (parent information packets)
3. Family help for schools and teachers (parent volunteers in the classroom)
4. Involvement in learning activities at home (a home-based Read-Aloud program)
5. Involvement in governance (a School–Parent Council)
6. Collaboration and exchange with the community (joint programs with community health centers).

See Davies, Burch, and Johnson (1992) for further examples within each area and case studies of six schools with comprehensive programs.

Several schools, districts, and even states are making efforts to initiate still more comprehensive programs in which the school would be the public site for the coordination of public health, mental health, educational, and recreational programs for the greater community, as suggested in Chapter 8. Kentucky, for example, has passed a statewide reform law establishing school-based health centers and parent councils at each school. Ed Zigler's (1987) School for the 21st Century model is in operation in six states and includes comprehensive early childhood, health, and educational services that are coordinated at the school level.

Elementary School P.S. 146 in East Harlem, New York, offers a huge array of services to children and families, which draw upon resources from city agencies, foundations, and corporations (Clinchy, 1992). A multidisciplinary committee called the School Based Support Staff runs workshops for parents, a bereavement group for students, a Models for Success program that brings to the school successful adults who have achieved against the odds, and an art club for students, teachers, and parents. A Big Brothers/Sisters Club supported in part by district funds develops student leadership in dealing with conflicts and provides mentoring for younger students. A program on nutrition and aerobics for families is offered in conjunction with Mount Sinai Medical Center. A national foundation is supporting an experiment in collaboration among three agencies: the Board of Education, the Human Resource Administration, and the Department of Parks and Recreation. In addition to providing the school with a social worker, youth recreation specialist, and parent activities coordinator, the collaboration has sparked programs such as a 7-week summer camp program and after-school programs for children and adults.

Key Elements in the Examples

For these more ambitious programs, several elements are crucial: imagining possibilities, orchestrating collaboration and inspiring commitment among diverse community partners, securing funding, and providing a framework for coordination and information sharing.

The leadership of the principal is indispensable, and usually a principal plays a key role in each of the functions described above. In general, the activities are sparked by a philosophy that considers family involvement a *necessary* component of children's school success.

In comprehensive programs that are based on partnership, mutual support and student's learning are generally equally important, and parents play a significant role in shaping the program.

Suggestions for Building Comprehensive Programs for Families

Assess Parents' Needs. When developing a large array of activities for families, a needs and interest assessment is crucial. As described in

Chapter 5, the methods of obtaining information from parents can vary: Questionnaires, telephone interviews with a sample of parents, focus groups, interviews in homes or in the community, and a targeted sample of parents to provide information over time can all be helpful. A combination of methods is often useful to reach diverse groups, such as parents who do not speak or read English, have no telephone, or do not have a permanent address. But because everyone is busy, it is important not to make this task too onerous or demanding: Collecting some information is better than collecting none, and small-scale initial efforts can be supplemented by later efforts. Regardless of the perfection of the process, if the desire for information is genuine and respectful and advice is heeded, parents are generally appreciative. Moreover, the process itself builds family interest in and commitment to subsequent activities. The experience of the coordinators of the School Based Support Staff at P.S. 146 capture the importance of a needs assessment process.

> When Cohen and Green started their parent workshops back in 1987, they had a tendency, they say, to decide by themselves what workshops would be about. Attendance was virtually nonexistent. When they instituted a turnabout and asked the parents what *they* wanted to talk about and the topics for the workshops were collaboratively brainstormed, attendance soared. (Clinchy, 1992, p. 31)

Coordinate Activities. When schools embark on an ambitious program of family outreach, coordination of activities is key. If schools do not invest in this role, continuity of effort cannot be maintained. Some schools coordinate activities through a teacher–parent committee, others by using a coordinator (who may be a parent, teacher, or community member). Coordinators need resources, a telephone, a private space, and time to accomplish all the liaison work and arrangements that are required. A stipend, release time, a salary, or other compensation for the coordinator(s) respects the importance of the work.

A frequent problem for the coordinators and for the school is that the development and implementation of family activities are divorced from the ongoing work of the school. A coordinator may do excellent work but have difficulty sharing information with the professional staff, building on classroom goals, and securing staff involvement in programs. A related problem is that the programs, though effective and enjoyable, may seem disconnected to each other and are not planned to build family or student strengths over time or establish increasingly close connections to school personnel (see Swap, 1990c).

The solution to both of these problems is the connection of family outreach activities to central school-based decision making (e.g., an SBM council subcommittee) and integration of the activities into the priorities of the school. These explicit connections emphasize the relationship of family outreach to school objectives and provide professional support and some clout to coordinator(s). Such coordination can occur without fundamental restructuring of the school.

Evaluate Programs. Another element of effective program development that is often overlooked is program evaluation. This component is not seen as important by many coordinators; and when time is short, the energy required to prepare, collect, and analyze evaluation data seems unproductive and burdensome. A principal captures this orientation very clearly: "One of the things that I've always put forward is if you worry about measures of success—if you spend your time figuring out what works and what didn't work—then that's time you could have spent *doing*. So what we do is do" (Thompson, 1991, p. 31).

In contrast, I feel that evaluation is essential to shape what is being done, to avoid repeating the same mistakes, and to develop connections and share learning with colleagues from other settings. Some training in commonsense evaluation procedures would be helpful for coordinators. But conviction that evaluation is useful is probably more important. My experience is that evaluation data are essential in designing future programs that are responsive to feedback. Memories fade quickly, and even remembering simple facts, such as how many people came to a particular session or what groups were not represented, becomes very difficult when a lot is going on. Data facilitate sharing information about the programs with others within and outside the school and are crucial for preserving and/or securing outside funding. Finally, when key personnel leave, data not only provide opportunities to celebrate what has occurred but also permit continuity of purpose and growth.

Build on Strengths. It is possible to build an ambitious network of programs for families based on a deficit model. In fact, as outlined in Chapter 3, many recent arguments in favor of school–community connections are based on the premise that some families will not become involved in their children's learning, and that the cultural capital that families do not provide can be obtained by encouraging students to participate in community offerings.

My experience suggests that programs that attempt to bypass families or are based on the premise that families are weak will not achieve partnership, unleash the enormous energy that parents have to support their children's school success, or overcome barriers to children's achievement.

PATH 3. RESTRUCTURING SCHOOLS FOR PARTNERSHIP AND STUDENT ACHIEVEMENT

Key Elements of Restructured Schools

In restructured schools that include parent involvement, building on parent strengths is explicit. Restructuring schools, discussed extensively in Chapter 9, is based on the collaboration of a community of learners who make decisions at the local level to achieve agreed upon goals. Parents are considered key members of the community, whose goals, skills, strengths, and efforts are *essential* to the planning and implementation of the goals.

Usually the importance of family involvement is set forth in the mission, objectives, or value statements of the school. Two-way communication and joint decision making are built into the model so that children's learning can be enhanced. As we have seen in Chapter 4, Levin's Accelerated School model seeks transformation based on three principles (unity of purpose, empowerment with accountability, and building on strengths) and seven values (equity, participation, communication/community, reflection, experimentation, trust, and risk-taking). Parent involvement is a major component of the reform, and parents are included in every aspect of the school program and school decision making. Comer's programs seek school transformation that is driven by the importance of strong, multifaceted relationships among children, parents, and educators. The management council and the staff support team reflect the commitment to joint decision making among parents and educators. As an example, P.S. 146 not only has comprehensive services for children and families, it is also a school committed to transformation of traditional school realities, as explained in its mission statement.

The mission of P.S. 146 is to use all resources to maximize the academic achievement of our children by improving the teaching/learning environment, through the ongoing collective and collaborative efforts of teachers, parents, and community. We know that we are in the business of education and can turn our children on to education so that they will continue learning for the rest of their lives.

- We believe that all our children can learn.
- We believe that we can effectively educate all our children.
- We believe we must act as advocates for our children.
- We believe that strong parent and community involvement is essential.
- We believe that we can achieve educational excellence.
- We believe that each child possesses unique talents and abilities, and we can help each child develop a feeling of self-worth and accomplishment.
- We believe we can create a school environment that will produce happy, secure, and well-adjusted children. (Clinchy, 1992, p. 29)

Another key element of restructured schools is that student outcomes are the focus of the mission. Conley (1991) defines restructuring as "activities that change fundamental assumptions, practices, and relationships, both within the organization and the outside world, in ways that lead to improved student learning outcomes" (p. 49). The Norfolk, Virginia, school district captured its commitment to restructuring with this mission statement: "All students will master the established educational objectives required for graduation with NO DIFFERENTIATION in the proportion of students demonstrating mastery of the essential educational objectives among the various socioeconomic levels" (Chrispeels, Henderson, Lezotte, & Madison, 1989, p. 5).

Suggestions for Initiating Restructuring

Plan a Sequence of Events. A sequential and spiraling model for family–school collaboration to improve students' learning would include the following steps:

1. School leaders announcing the importance of partnerships to achieve student success and engaging in activities to build relationships between educators and families
2. Inviting families and community members to join in developing the school's mission and goals
3. Selecting a school council (composed of parents, educators, community members, and students at the secondary level) to make school decisions
4. The council appointing task forces to pursue 2–4 agreed upon priorities based on an analysis of data on school achievement patterns and an assessment of achievable goals
5. The council approving and monitoring activities, structures, and programs to improve student achievement and enhance home–

school partnerships initiated by the task forces or other members of the community

6. The council evaluating progress in meeting goals and reflecting on this information with the community at regular intervals
7. The council planning next steps based on results to date, conferring with constituent groups, and re-examining priorities. As appropriate, the council would return to step 4, in order to continue with existing priorities or develop new ones.
8. The council also periodically reviewing its own process and developing procedures to expand opportunities for participation in the community (a return to step 1). (See Swap, 1991, for further elaboration.)

Select a Framework for Action. A council or study group that is focused on improving partnerships needs to frame two questions for itself: What model of partnership will guide our activities? and What goals will we pursue? A group of parents and educators that is representative of the school can pursue these questions through readings, visits to other sites, and conversations with consultants. It is very important to present the results of the group's deliberations to the school community as a whole so that they can review the work, reshape it as appropriate, and develop consensus about direction. The group that is selected to initiate and coordinate activities ahould communicate regularly with the community as a whole through an SBM Council (or equivalent), community meetings, and informal channels.

Build Readiness Among Faculty. Although individual faculty might be in many different stages of readiness for experimentation in a given school, most settings do not try to achieve restructuring without the consent of a majority. As mentioned earlier, faculty readiness for the challenge of restructuring develops from the modeling provided by others, incentives of various kinds, professional development activities, and new successes in teaching.

Commit to a 3 to 5 year Process. Transformation of a school is obviously a complex and challenging enterprise. It is important to realize that uneven progress and setbacks are the norm. Optimism, hard work, patience, and alacrity in celebrating small and large successes are needed. There are no "quick fixes" available when the task is changing longstanding patterns of relationships and behaviors: A multi-year, renewable commitment is essential at the outset.

Consider Long-Term Consultation. Training for the principal and council members would be helpful at many junctures, for the several purposes mentioned in Chapter 9. In my experience, the services of a consultant to the school would be optimally helpful at certain key points in this sequence, such as deciding how to structure the community discussion to decide about mission and priorities; determining how to define the initial roles, relationships, and process of the steering committee; learning how to collect and use data to shape an inquiry process; learning how to set priorities that are ambitious and exciting but also responsive to the realities and resources of the participants; and helping the group to work through the first few inevitable crises. Given the restriction of resources in most schools, it is wise to consider taking advantage of resources for consultation within the community and among professional peers engaged in complementary efforts. A general strategy would be to use expert help just to frame problems and develop internal expertise.

Secure and Widen District Support. As we reviewed in Chapter 5, active district support through congruent policies, financial incentives, and public commitment is helpful if not essential. Local school personnel should seek this commitment and keep central office personnel aware of problems, progress, needs, and celebrations.

Recognize Uniqueness. Having identified a general sequence of activities for restructuring, it is also necessary to point out that no two efforts develop in exactly the same way. The uniqueness of each community shapes the opportunities and constraints of the process. It is wise to have a path in mind, but to take advantage of serendipity, revising expectations and priorities based on events and experiences.

SUMMARY

Despite the rhetoric supporting home–school partnerships, there is a lack of coherent policy, significant resources, national standards, and professional preparation that would support those who are committed to implementing them. Nonetheless, those interested in initiating partnerships can identify useful ideas and practices by learning about schools that are developing effective outreach to families.

In this chapter, we examined three paths to partnership, each of which draws upon the elements of partnership outlined earlier in this book: establishing two-way communication, providing mutual support, enhancing learning at home and school, and making joint decisions. The three paths described required increasing levels of commitment and were defined as (1) establishing limited partnerships for student learning, (2) building comprehensive networks of services for families, and (3) restructuring schools for partnership and student learning.

In the sections on limited partnerships and comprehensive services, we reviewed program options, key elements, and suggestions for avoiding common problems. In the section on restructuring, which had already been introduced in Chapter 9, a sequence of steps for increasing student achievement and family involvement was outlined, and suggestions were made for using consultants judiciously and broadening participation.

CONCLUSION

The crisis in American education has created widespread disequilibrium. We are concerned about high levels of school failure, and we worry that traditional teaching methods and curriculum are inadequate to respond to the increasingly diverse needs of our children. Although we know that family involvement in children's education increases achievement, differences in values and expectations between families and educators have made collaboration difficult.

Yet crisis often creates opportunity. Because disequilibrium is so widespread, there is energy and motivation in many sites to transform traditional schooling. This book has described many of these experimental efforts to transform the culture of the school and to redefine its boundaries, processes, and outcomes to include families. Further initiatives to reshape home–school partnerships and to improve student outcomes are yet to be discovered. Reframing the school culture as a community of learners dedicated to success for all children creates a context in which many new insights can be generated. I hope that the conceptual frameworks and suggestions for action offered in this book provide both impetus and support for answering the questions: "And should I then presume?/And how should I begin?" Your efforts are needed.

References

Anderson, J. (1988). *The education of blacks in the South, 1860–1935*. Chapel Hill: University of North Carolina Press.

Aronstein, W., Marlow, M., & Desilets, B. (1990). Detours on the road to site-based management. *Educational Leadership, 47*(7), 61–63.

Auerbach, E. R. (1989). Toward a social-contextual approach to family literacy. *Harvard Educational Review, 59*(2), 165–181.

Bacon, K. (1990, July 31). Many educators view involved parents as key to children's success in school. *Wall Street Journal*, p. B1.

Bailey, W. (1991). *School-site management applied*. Lancaster, PA: Technomic Publishing Co.

Barr, D., & Cochran, M. (1992). Understanding and supporting empowerment: Redefining the professional role. *Networking Bulletin, 2*(3), 1–8.

Barth, R. (1991). *Improving schools from within*. San Francisco: Jossey-Bass.

Bauch, J. (1989). The Trans*Parent* school model: New technology for parent involvement. *Educational Leadership, 47*(2), 32–34.

Benjamin, L. (1992). *The Black elite*. Chicago: Nelson-Hall Publishers.

Berrueta-Clement, J., Schweinhart, L., Barnett, W., Epstein, A., & Weikart, D. (1984). *Changed lives: The effects of the Perry Preschool Project on youths through age 19*. Ypsilanti, MI: High Scope Press.

Brammer, L. (1988). *The helping relationship: Process and skills* (4th ed.). Englewood Cliffs, NJ: Prentice-Hall.

Brandt, R. (1989). On improving school and family connections: A conversation with Joyce Epstein. *Educational Leadership, 47*(2), 24–27.

Brandt, R. (1992). On rethinking leadership: A conversation with Tom Sergiovanni. *Educational Leadership, 49*(5), 46–49.

Braun, L., & Swap, S. (1987). *Building home-school partnerships with America's changing families*. Boston: Wheelock College.

Brinckerhoff, J., & Vincent, L. (1986). Increasing parental decision-making at the Individualized Educational Program meeting. *Journal of the Division for Early Childhood, 11*(1), 46–58.

Bronfenbrenner, U. (1974). *Is early intervention effective? A report on longitudinal evaluations of preschool programs* (Vol. 2). Washington, DC: Department of Health, Education, and Welfare.

Brown, L. (1991). *Results of survey on pre-service teacher education practices in parent–teacher conferencing*. Paper available from the Author, Education Department, Clarion University of Pennsylvania, Clarion, PA 16214.

Burns, L., & Howes, J. (1990, August). Handing control to local schools: Site-based management sweeps the country. *The School Administrator*, pp. 8–18.

Carle, E. (1989). *The very hungry caterpillar.* Cleveland: Collins-World (Original work published 1970).

Carnegie Forum on Education and the Economy. (1986). *A nation prepared: Teachers for the 21st century.* Report of the Carnegie Task Force on Teaching as a Profession. Washington, DC: Author.

Chall, J., & Snow, C. (1982, Dec. 22). *Families and literacy: The contributions of out-of-school experiences to children's acquisition of literacy.* A final report to the National Institute of Education. Cambridge, MA: Harvard University. (ERIC Document Reproduction Service No. ED 234 345)

Children's Defense Fund. (1989). *A vision for America's future.* Washington, DC: Author.

Chinn, P., & Hughes, S. (1987). Representation of minority students in special education classes. *Remedial and Special Education, 8*(4), 41–46.

Chrispeels, J. (1991). District leadership in parent involvement. *Phi Delta Kappan, 72*(5), 367–371.

Chrispeels, J., Fernandez, B., & Preston, J. (1990). *Home and school: Partners for student success: A Handbook for principals.* San Diego, CA: San Diego City Schools.

Chrispeels, J., Henderson, A., Lezotte, L., & Madison, A. (1989, Summer). Effective school-based improvement: Two case studies. *Network for Public Schools, 14*(6), 3–5, 14.

Clark, R. (1983). *Family life and school achievement: Why poor black children succeed or fail.* Chicago: University of Chicago Press.

Clinchy, E. (1992). Building an extended family in East Harlem. *Equity and Choice, 8*(2), 28–34.

Cochran, M. (1987). The parental empowerment process: Building on strengths. *Equity and Choice, 4*(1), 9–23.

Coleman, J. (1989). The family, the community, and the future of education. In W. Weston (Ed.). *Education and the American family: A research synthesis* (pp. 169–185). New York: New York University Press.

Coleman, J. (1991). *Parental involvement in education* (Order No. 065-000-00459-3). Washington, DC: U.S. Government Printing Office.

College Board Publications. (no date). *Getting into the equation.* New York: Author.

Collins, C., Moles, O., & Cross, M. (1982). *The home–school connection: Selected partnership programs in large cities.* Boston: Institute for Responsive Education.

Comer, J. (1980). *School power.* New York: Free Press.

Comer, J. (1988a). Educating poor minority children. *Scientific American, 259*(5), 42–48.

Comer, J. (1988b). Is "parenting" essential to good teaching? *NEA Today, 6,* 34–40.

Comer, J. (1988c). *Maggie's American dream.* New York: New American Library.

Conley, D. (1991). What is restructuring? Educators adapt to a changing world. *Equity and Choice, 7*(2 & 3), 46–55.

Cuban, L. (1988). A fundamental puzzle of school reform. *Phi Delta Kappan*, *69*(5), 341–344.

Cutright, M. (1989). *The National PTA Talks to Parents: How to get the best education for your child*. New York: Doubleday.

David, J. (1989). Synthesis of research on school-based management. *Educational Leadership*, *46*(8), 45–53.

David, J. (1991). What it takes to restructure education. *Educational Leadership*, *48*(8), 11–15.

Davies, D. (1988). Low-income parents and the schools: A research report and a plan for action. *Equity and Choice*, *4*(3), 51–59.

Davies, D. (1990a). Schools Reaching Out: Family, school, and community partnerships for student success. *Phi Delta Kappan*, *72*(5), 376–382.

Davies, D. (1990b). *Schools Reaching Out: What have we learned? A final report: Part I*. Boston: Institute for Responsive Education.

Davies, D., Burch, P., & Johnson, V. (1992). *A portrait of Schools Reaching Out*. Boston: Center on Families, Communities, Schools, and Children's Learning.

Delpit, L. (1986). Skills and other dilemmas of a progressive black educator. *Harvard Educational Review*, *56*(4), 379–385.

Delpit, L. (1988). The silenced dialogue: Power and pedgogy in educating other people's children. *Harvard Educational Review*, *58*(3), 280–298.

Dinkmeyer, D., & McKay, G. (1976). *STEP (Systematic training for effective parenting)*. Circle Pines, MN: American Guidance Service.

Dornbusch, S., & Ritter, P. (1988). Parents of high school students: A neglected resource. *Educational Horizons*, *66*, 75–77.

Duncan, L. (1969). Parent–counselor conferences make a difference. St. Petersburg, FL: St. Petersburg Junior College. (ERIC Document Reproduction Service No. ED 031 743)

Edelman, M. (1992). *The measure of our success: A letter to my children and yours*. Boston: Beacon Press.

Edwards, P. (1990). *Parents as partners in reading*. Chicago: Children's Press.

Eliot, T. S. (1963). *T. S. Eliot: Collected poems: 1909–1962*. New York: Harcourt, Brace, and World.

Elmore, R., & Associates. (1991). *Restructuring schools: The next generation of educational reform*. San Francisco: Jossey-Bass.

Epstein, J. (1985). Home and school connections in schools of the future: Implications of research on parent involvement. *Peabody Journal of Education*, *62*(2), 18–41.

Epstein, J. (1987). Parent involvement: What research says to administrators. *Education and Urban Society*, *19*(2), 119–136.

Epstein, J. (1990). School and family connections: Theory, research, and implications for integrating sociologies of education and family. In D. Unger & M. Sussman (Eds.), *Families in community settings: Interdisciplinary perspectives* (pp. 99–126). New York: Haworth Press.

Epstein, J. (1991a). Effects of teacher practices of parent involvement on change in student achievement in reading and math. In S. Silvern (Ed.), *Literacy through family, community, and school interaction* (pp. 261–276). Greenwich, CT: JAI Press.

Epstein, J. (Ed.). (1991b). Paths to partnership: What we can learn from federal, state, district, and local initiatives [Special section]. *Phi Delta Kappan, 72*(5), 344–386.

Epstein, J., & associates. (1992). *Teachers Involve Parents in Schoolwork (TIPS): Manuals for teachers and prototype activities for the elementary and middle grades.* Baltimore: Center on Families, Communities, Schools and Children's Learning, Johns Hopkins University.

Epstein, J., & Becker, H. (1982). Teachers' reported practices of parent involvement: Problems and possibilities. *Elementary School Journal, 83*, 103–114.

Epstein, J., & Dauber, S. (1991). School programs and teacher practices of parent involvement in inner-city elementary and middle schools. *Elementary School Journal, 91*, 289–303.

First, J., & Carrera, J. (1988). *New voices: Immigrant students in U.S. public schools.* Boston: National Coalition of Advocates for Students.

Fisher, R., & Ury, W. (1981). *Getting to yes.* Boston: Houghton-Mifflin.

Freedman, S., Aschheim, B., Zerchykov, R., & Frank, R. (1989). *Focus on parents: Strategies for increasing the involvement of underrepresented families in education.* Quincy: Office of Community Education, Massachusetts Department of Education.

Freedman, S., Aschheim, B., Zerchykov, R., & Frank, R. (1990). *Parent–school collaboration: A compendium of strategies for parent involvement.* Quincy: Office of Community Education, Massachusetts Department of Education.

Gibbs, T. (1990, October 8). Shameful bequests to the next generation. *Time,* pp. 42–46.

Goldsmith, E., & Handel, R. (1990). *Family reading.* New York: New Readers Press.

Goode, D. (1990). The community portrait process: School–community collaboration. *Equity and Choice, 6*(3), 32–37.

Goodlad, J. (1984). *A place called school: Prospects for the future.* New York: McGraw-Hill.

Gordon, T. (1975). *P.E.T.: Parent Effectiveness Training.* New York: New American Library.

Gotts, E. (1980). Long-term effects of a home-oriented preschool program. *Childhood Education, 56*, 228–234.

Greene, G., & Habana-Hafner, S. (1988). *Handbook on home–school collaboration.* Quincy: Massachusetts Department of Education.

Hafner, A. (1990). A profile of the American eighth grader: NELS:88 student descriptive summary. Washington, DC: National Center for Education Statistics.

Hagstrom, D. (1992). Alaska's discovery school. *Educational Leadership, 49*(5), 23–26.

Hauser-Cram, J. (1983). *A question of balance: Relationships between teachers and parents.* Doctoral dissertation, Harvard Graduate School of Education.

Hawley, W. (1989). The importance of minority teachers to the racial and ethical integration of American society. *Equity and Choice, 5*(2), 31–36.

Heath, S. (1983). *Ways with words: Language, life, and work in communities and classrooms.* Cambridge: Cambridge University Press.

Heath, S., & McLaughlin, M. (1987). A child resource policy: Moving beyond dependence on school and family. *Phi Delta Kappan, 68*(8), 576–580.

Henderson, A. (1981). *Parent participation and student achievement: The evidence grows.* Columbia, MD: National Committee for Citizens in Education.

Henderson, A. (1987). *The evidence continues to grow: Parent involvement improves student achievement.* Columbia, MD: National Committee for Citizens in Education.

Hess, R., & Azuma, H. (1991). Cultural support for schooling: Contrasts between Japan and the United States. *Educational Researcher, 20*(9), 2–8, 12.

Hess, R., & Shipman, V. (1965). Early experience and the socialization of cognitive modes in children. *Child Development, 36,* 869–886.

Hidalgo, N. (1992). *"I saw puerto rico once": A review of the literature on Puerto Rican families in the United States.* Boston: Center on Families, Communities, Schools, and Children's Learning.

Hobbs, N. (1984). *Strengthening families.* San Francisco: Jossey-Bass.

Home and School Institute. (1984). *In any language: Parents are teachers: Grades 4–6.* Washington, DC: Author.

Home and School Institute. (1987). *Survival guide for busy parents: Help children do well at school while you do well on the job.* Washington, DC: Author.

Hopfenberg, W., Levin, H., Meister, G., & Rogers, J. (1990). *Towards accelerated middle schools for at-risk youth.* CERAS 402S, School of Education, Stanford University, Stanford, CA 94305.

Irujo, S. (1989). Do you know why they all talk at once? Thoughts on cultural differences between Hispanics and Anglos. *Equity and Choice, 5*(3), 14–18.

Jackson, B., & Cooper, B. (1989). Parent choice and empowerment: New roles for parents. *Urban Education, 24*(3), 263–286.

Jackson, B., Davies, D., Cooper, B., & Page, J. (1988). *Parents make a difference: An evaluation of the New York City Schools' 1987–1988 parent involvement program.* Report to the New York City Public Schools. New York: Fordham University Graduate School of Education and Boston: Institute for Responsive Education.

Jennings, W. (1989). How to organize successful parent advisory committees. *Eductional Leadership, 47*(2), 42–45.

Jensen, A. (1969). How much can we boost IQ and scholastic achievement? *Harvard Education Review, 39*(1), 1–123.

Johnson, V. (1990). Schools Reaching Out: Changing the message to "good news." *Equity and Choice, 6*(3), 20–24.

Joyce, B., Bennett, B., & Rolheiser-Bennett, C. (1990). The self-educating teacher: Empowering teachers through research. In B. Joyce (Ed.), *Changing school culture through staff development, 1990 Yearbook* (pp. 26–40). Alexandria, VA: Association for Supervision and Curriculum Development.

Kagan, S. (1989). Early care and education: Beyond the schoolhouse doors. *Phi Delta Kappan, 71*(2), 107–112.

Kidder, T. (1989). *Among school children.* Boston: Houghton Mifflin.

Kijai, J., & Norman, J. (1990). *The status and impact of school improvement councils.* Columbia: School Council Assistance Project, College of Education, University of South Carolina.

Krasnow, J. (1990a). *Building parent–teacher partnerships: Prospects from the perspective of the Schools Reaching Out project.* Boston: Institute for Responsive Education.

Krasnow, J. (1990b). *Improving family–school relationships: Teacher research from the Schools Reaching Out project.* Boston: Institute for Responsive Education.

Lawrence Hall of Science. (1979). *Family Math.* University of California at Berkeley, Berkeley, CA 94720.

Leitch, M., & Tangri, S. (1988). Barriers to home–school collaboration. *Educational Horizons, 66,* 70–74.

Lerman, S. (1983). *Responsive parenting series.* Circle Pines, MN: American Guidance Service.

Levin, H. (1987). Accelerated schools for disadvantaged students. *Educational Leadership, 44*(6), 19–21.

Levin, H. (1988a). Accelerating elementary education for disadvantaged students. In Council of Chief State Officers (Ed.), *School success for children at risk* (pp. 209–226). San Diego, CA: Harcourt Brace Jovanovich.

Levin, H. (1988b, November 17–18). Don't remediate: Accelerate. In *Conference papers* (pp. 2–3) prepared for the Stanford University Centennial Conference.

Levine, M. (1992). *Professional practice schools: Linking teacher education and school reform.* New York: Teachers College Press.

Lightfoot, S. (1978). *Worlds apart: Relationships between families and schools.* New York: Basic Books.

Locust, C. (1988). Wounding the spirit: Discrimination and traditional American Indian belief systems. *Harvard Educational Review, 58*(3), 315–330.

Love, M. (1989). The home visit: An irreplaceable tool. *Educational Leadership, 47*(2), 29.

Malen, B., & Ogawa, R. (1988). Professional–patron influence on site-based governance councils: A confounding case study. *Educational Evaluation and Policy Analysis, 10*(4), 251–270.

Marburger, C. (1985). *One school at a time: School-based management, a process for change.* Columbia, MD: National Committee for Citizens in Education.

Mason: A little school that can. (1991, October). *SchoolWorks, 1*(1), 1, 3.

Massachusetts Department of Education. (1990). *Parents-as-teachers: A statewide and national resource guide.* Quincy, MA: Author.

McCarty, T., Wallace, S., Lynch, R., & Benally, A. (1991). Classroom inquiry and Navajo learning styles: A call for reassessment. *Anthropology and Education Quarterly, 22,* 42–57.

McLaughlin, M., & Shields, P. (1987). Involving low-income parents in the schools: A role for policy? *Phi Delta Kappan, 69*(2), 156–160.

Mehran, M., & White, K. (1988). Parent tutoring as a supplement to compensatory education for first-grade children. *Remedial and Special Education, 9*(3), 35–41.

Moles, O. (1982). Synthesis of recent research on parent participation in children's education. *Educational Leadership, 40*(2), 44–47.

Moles, O. (1992). *Schools and families together: Helping children learn more at home.* Washington, DC: Office of Research, OERI, U.S. Dept. of Education, 20208.

Moses, R., Kamii, M., Swap, S., & Howard, J. (1989). The Algebra Project: Organizing in the spirit of Ella. *Harvard Educational Review, 59*(4), 423–443.

Murphy, J. (1987). *The School Development program: (The "Comer Process").* Prince George's County, MD: Prince George's County Public Schools.

Murphy, J. (1992). *Restructuring schools.* New York: Teachers College Press.

National Association of Partners in Education. (no date). *Your child can be a super reader.* Alexandria, VA: Author.

National Center for Health Statistics. (1991). Advance report of final natality statistics, 1989. *Monthly Vital Statistics Report, 40*(8). Hyattsville, MD: Public Health Service.

National Institute of Education. (no date). *Help your child do better in school.* Washington, DC: Author.

National PTA. (1989). *Math matters: Kids are counting on you.* Chicago: Author.

National School Volunteer Program. (1979). *Handbook for teachers: Effective involvement of school volunteers.* Alexandria, VA: Author.

Nelson-Barber, S., & Meier, T. (1990, Spring). Multicultural context a key factor in teaching. *Academic Connections,* Office of Academic Affairs, The College Board, pp. 1–5, 9–11.

Noddings, N. (1988). An ethic of care and its implications for instructional arrangements. *American Journal of Education, 96*(2), 219–230.

O'Connell, M. (1991). School reform, Chicago style: How citizens organized to change public policy [Special issue of *The Neighborhood Works*]. Chicago: Center for Neighborhood Technology.

Office of Educational Research and Improvement. (no date). *Help your child become a good reader.* Washington, DC: Author.

Office of Educational Research and Improvement. (no date). *Help your child improve in test-taking.* Washington, DC: Author.

Office of Educational Research and Improvement. (no date). *Help your child learn to write well.* Washington, DC: Author.

Ogbu, J. (1983). Minority status and schooling in plural societies. *Comparative Educational Review, 6,* 168–190.

Ogbu, J. (1990). Overcoming racial barriers to equal access. In J. Goodlad (Ed.), *Access to knowledge* (pp. 59–90). New York: College Entrance Examination Board.

Okakok, L. (1989). Serving the purpose of education. *Harvard Educational Review, 59*(4), 405–422.

Olmstead, P., & Rubin, R. (1983). Linking parent behaviors to child achievement: Four evaluation studies from the Parent Education Follow Through programs. *Studies in Educational Evaluation, 8,* 317–325.

O'Neill, J. (1990). Piecing together the restructuring puzzle. *Educational Leadership, 47*(7), 4–10.

Ooms, T. (1992). *Family-school partnership: A critical component of school reform.* Background briefing report for seminar held in February 1992. Washington, DC: Family Impact Seminar, The American Association for Marriage and Family Therapy.

Pang, V. (1988). Ethnic prejudice: Still alive and hurtful. *Harvard Educational Review, 58*(3), 375–379.

Perry, T. (1990, April). *Re-visioning teacher preparation: Teachers and the new common culture.* Paper presented at the annual conference of the American Educational Research Association, Boston.

Perry, T. (1992). *The search for a theoretical perspective on African American school achievement* (first draft). Boston: Center on Families, Communities, Schools, and Children's Learning.

Perry, T., & Fraser, J. (1993). *Freedom's plough: Teaching in the multicultural classroom.* New York: Rutledge Press.

Ribadeneira, D. (1990, June 12). Roxbury school breaks the mold on learning. *The Boston Globe,* pp. 1, 16.

Rich, D. (1988). *MegaSkills: How families can help children succeed in school and beyond.* Boston: Houghton Mifflin.

Richards, J. (1993). Classroom tapestry: A practitioner's perspective on multicultural education. In T. Perry & J. Fraser (Eds.), *Freedom's plough: Teaching in the multicultural classroom.* New York: Routledge.

Role of the national center. (1992). *Accelerated Schools, 2*(2), 14–15.

Rothman, R. (1992, March 4). Denver schools, board in "power struggle" over testing policy. *Education Week,* p. 5.

Sambs, C., & Schenkat, R. (1990). One district learns about restructuring. *Educational Leadership, 47*(7), 72–75.

Sattes, B. (1985). *Parent involvement: A review of the literature* (Occasional Paper No. 21). Charleston, WV: Appalachia Educational Laboratory.

Schlechty, P. (1991). *Schools for the 21st century: Leadership imperatives for educational reform.* San Francisco: Jossey-Bass.

Schorr, L. (1988). *Within our reach: Breaking the cycle of disadvantage.* New York: Doubleday/Anchor.

Scollon, R., & Scollon, S. (1981). *Narrative, literacy, and face in interethnic communication.* Norwood, NJ: Ablex Publishing.

Seeley, D. (1985). *Education through partnership.* Washington, DC: American Enterprise Institute for Public Policy Research.

Seeley, D. (1989). A new paradigm for parent involvement. *Educational Leadership, 47*(2), 46–48.

Sege, I. (1990, September 2). '90 Census indicates immigrants restocking melting pot. *The Boston Globe*, pp. 1, 18.

Sirotnik, K., & Goodlad, J. (Eds.). (1988). *School-university partnerships in action*. New York: Teachers College Press.

Siu, S. (1992). *Toward an understanding of Chinese-American educational achievement: A literature review*. Boston: Center on Families, Communities, Schools, and Children's Learning. Report No. 2.

Sommerfeld, M. (1992, April 15). National commitment to parent role in schools sought. *Education Week*, pp. 1, 11.

South Carolina State Department of Education. (1985). *Setting up the school volunteer program*, Columbia, SC: EDRS# ED232887.

Strathclyde Regional Council. (1990). *Pre-5 unit: Policy principles and information*. Glasgow, Scotland: Department of Education.

Swap, S. (1987). *Enhancing parent involvement in schools*. New York: Teachers College Press.

Swap, S. (1990a). Comparing three models of home-school collaboration. *Equity and Choice, 6*(3), 9-19.

Swap, S. (1990b). *Parent involvement and success for all children: What we know now*. Boston: Institute for Responsive Education.

Swap, S. (1990c). *Schools Reaching Out and success for all children: Two case studies*. Boston: Institute for Responsive Education.

Swap, S. (1991). How can we crack the achievement barrier in urban schools? *Equity and Choice, 7*(2 & 3), 58-64.

Swap, S., & Krasnow, J. (1992). *A saga of Irish-American achievement: Constructing a positive identity*. Boston: Center on Families, Communities, Schools, and Children's Learning.

Taylor, D., & Dorsey-Gaines, E. (1988). *Growing up literate: Learning from inner-city families*. Portsmouth, NH: Heinemann.

Thompson, S. (1991). Testing goodness: An interview with Steven C. Leonard, Principal, Martin Luther King, Jr. Middle School. *Equity and Choice, 7*(1 & 2), 31-34.

Thornton, S. (1990). *Building the bridge to tomorrow*. Sacramento: California Department of Education.

Timar, T. (1989). The politics of school restructuring. *Phi Delta Kappan, 71*(4), 265-275.

Tizard, J., Schofield, W., & Hewison, J. (1982). Collaboration between teachers and parents in assisting children's reading. *British Journal of Educational Psychology, 52*(1), 1-11.

Trovato, J., & Bucher, B. (1980). Peer tutoring with or without home-based reinforcement, for reading remediation. *Journal of Applied Behavioral Analysis, 13*(1), 129-141.

Turnbull, A., & Turnbull, H. (1990). *Families, professionals, and exceptionality: A special partnership* (2nd ed.). Columbus, OH: Merrill.

Utterback, P., & Kalin, M. (1989). A community-based model of curriculum evaluation. *Educational Leadership, 47*(2), 49-50.

Vogler, D., & Hutchins, D. (1988). *Parents as tutors: Minimizing the homework hassle*. Alexandria, VA: National Community Education Association.

Walberg, H., Bole, R., & Waxman, H. (1980). School-based family socialization and reading achievement in the inner-city. *Psychology in the Schools, 17*, 509–514.

Warner, I. (1991). Parents in touch: District leadership for parent involvement. *Phi Delta Kappan, 72*(5), 372–375.

Wheelock, A. (1990). *Locked in/locked out: Tracking and placement practices in Boston Public Schools, A report*. Boston: Massachusetts Advocacy Center.

Williams, M. (1989). *Neighborhood organizing for urban school reform*. New York: Teachers College Press.

Yao, E. (1985). Adjustment needs of Asian immigrant children. *Elementary School Guidance and Counseling, 19*, 222–228.

Yao, E. (1988). Working effectively with Asian immigrant parents. *Phi Delta Kappan, 70*(3), 223–225.

Zacchei, D., & Mirman, J. (1986). *Business–education partnerships*. Andover, MA: Regional Laboratory for Educational Improvement of the Northeast and Islands.

Zeldin, S. (1990). *Organizational structures and interpersonal relations: Policy implications for Schools Reaching Out*. Boston: Institute for Responsive Education.

Zigler, E. (1987, October). A solution to the nation's child care crisis: The school of the twenty-first century. Parents as Teachers National Center, *Investing in the Beginning* (pp. 27–33). Conference Report, St. Louis, MO.

APPENDIX A: CHILD PROFILE

AMBROSE SCHOOL
CHILD PROFILE

This optional profile has been developed to provide the teacher
with a better understanding of your child. The questions asked are
completely voluntary in whole or in part. The profile will be
returned to you at the end of the school year. You can resubmit
this form the following year or complete a new one.

Child's Name: _____Nickname:_____

Date of Birth: _____Current Age:_____ Grade:_____

1. Parents: **Mother**   **Father**
   Name: _____   _____
   Occupation: _____   _____
   Place of
    Employ: _____   _____
   Daytime
    Phone: _____   _____

2. List all the children in the family in chronological order,
beginning with the oldest:
   Name   **Sex**   **Age**
   _____   _____   _____
   _____   _____   _____
   _____   _____   _____
   _____   _____   _____
   _____   _____   _____

3. Adults living in the child's household include:
   ____mother   ____grandmother   ____other adult relative
   ____father   ____grandfather   ____nonrelated caregiver
   ____step-parent

4. Is your child able to speak or understand a language other than
   English?_____ If so, please specify:_____

5. Please list any other schools your child attended before coming
   to Ambrose:_____
   _____

6. For each of the areas listed below, please note information that
   you feel would help the teacher to understand and work with your
   child. (You may continue on the back of this page.)

   a) Child's strengths:

   b) Child's interests and after-school activities:

Reprinted with permission from Dr. Richard Rogers, Principal, Ambrose School, Winchester, Massachusetts.

   c) Personality and/or behavioral characteristics (e.g., feelings
      about school, nervousness, shyness, competitiveness,
      impulsiveness, activity level, etc.)

   d) Recent family events or changes (e.g., death, divorce, new
      sibling, moving, etc.)

   e) Areas of academic difficulty or concern:

   f) Relationship with peers:

7. Are there any goals or expectations you have set or would like
   to set with your child this year?

8. How do you feel the teacher can best support your child's
   learning this year?

9. Are there any areas in which you as a parent would like to
   become involved in the classroom or school?

10. Is there anything you think your child would like the teacher
    to know about her/him?

**Please attach any additional comments or suggestions on a separate
page.**

This profile was completed by_____
                       Date:_____

APPENDIX B: FAMILY INFORMATION FORM

PROMISING PRACTICE: DEVELOPING A FAMILY INFORMATION FORM

PROBLEM: Julie C., Principal of the Lake Avenue School, a private elementary school, was aware that large numbers of children in the school lived with single parents, in joint custody arrangements, and/or in blended families. In fact, the number of children in single parent families and step-families outnumbered those in traditional two-parent families. Julie believed that it was important to reach out to all the significant adults in a child's life, but she found that it was difficult for the school to know who those people were. Parents did not routinely volunteer the information, and teachers did not want to appear to be prying.

STRATEGY: Julie decided to develop an office information form that would give the school the necessary information without antagonizing parents. Here's what she did.

Determining the Content

In a written memo, Julie asked her staff members to think about what information they would like to have about the families of the children they taught. The information should be useful to them in working with the children and in reaching out to parents; it should not be information to satisfy curiosity.

At the next staff meeting, the teachers shared their lists and after some discussion, agreed on the most important information to them: the names and addresses of both parents; the names and relationship of other adults living with the child; who should receive school mailings, report cards, and invitations to conferences, etc., and what adults have permission to pick up the child at school.

Developing the Form

On the basis of this information, Julie and some staff members put together the first draft of a general office information form.

Checking with Parents

At the next parent board meeting, Julie explained what she wanted to do, described the kind of content the teachers had agreed would be helpful, and asked for comment on the draft form she had developed. The board discussed it and suggested some minor changes.

Julie then wrote a paragraph in the school newsletter, informing parents that a new information form was being developed and inviting any interested parent to contact her if he/she wished to review the draft.

Reprinted with permission from Braun, L., & Swap, S. (1987). *Building home-school partnerships with America's changing families*. Boston, MA: Wheelock College.

Implementation

Julie took the various suggestions she had received and developed a final draft of the form. She shared it with teachers at their next staff meeting and with parents at their next board meeting. Both groups supported her efforts. In early September, the parents of all children were asked to fill out and return the following form.

LAKE AVENUE SCHOOL
General Office Information

Child's Residence	Other Parent's Residence
_____	_____
Child's Name	Name
_____	_____
Name(s) of Parent(s)	Street
_____	_____
Street	Town and Zip
_____	_____
Town and Zip	Phone
_____	_____
Phone (home and work)	Work Phone

Please note that all mailings are sent to both parents unless
otherwise indicated. If mailings ARE NOT to be mailed to BOTH
parents, please indicate below.

_____	_____
Parent's signature	Parent's signature

Other adults

It is sometimes helpful to us to know about other significant
adults in a child's life (grandparents, step-parents, special
friends, etc.). Please feel free to fill in the section below
if it is relevant.

Other adults living in child's residence

_____	_____
Name	Relationship to child
_____	_____
Name	Relationship to child

Other Parent's Residence

_____	_____
Name	Relationship to child
_____	_____
Name	Relationship to child

Please share other information you think we should know. (You
may use the reverse, if needed.) Thank you.

Transportation

My child will be traveling to and from school by: _____

If by regular cab or school bus company, please list the name of company or driver and phone number. _____

_____

If your child will be picked up after school, please list the people who have your permission to do so.

_____   _____

_____   _____

The school will not allow others to pick up your child without your permission. Please notify the office of any change in arrangments.

Other Information
(from previous page)

APPENDIX C: PARENT INTEREST FORM, PARENT ATTITUDE SURVEY

Kindergarten Parents' Interest Form

Dear Parents of Follow Through Kindergarten children,
    Several parents and teachers have begun to think about a parent program for the Kindergarten classes. We feel that different parents will have different ideas about what they would like to do. We want to know your ideas. Please check the activities you might like to participate in and send this survey to your child's teachers by the end of the week. We will share the results of this survey at our next parent meeting in October.

Working with the children:

___celebrating your child's birthday in school

——reading stories

——making books

——cooking

——using simple wood tools

——sharing your ethnic heritage

——sewing

——doing art projects

——making music

___taking a small group to visit your place of work

___taking a small group on a neighborhood walk

Other ideas?_____

Helping the teachers:

___making games at home for school use

___picking out books at the library

___getting items needed for class projects

___sending in food for healthy afternoon snacks

___preparing materials at school (dittos, bookmaking...)

——helping supervise recess (1:00-2:00)

——filling in for an absent teacher

——going on field trips

——driving others on field trips

——helping supervise lunch (10:40-11:10)

Other ideas?_____

Getting together with other parents:

___discussion groups with a leader

___support groups just for parents

——social events

Other ideas?_____

Possible topics:

——reading in Kindergarten

——math in Kindergarten

——single parenting

——child development from 4 to 6 yrs.

——discipline

——building self-confidence in children

PLEASE ADD ANY OTHER IDEAS ON THE BACK OF THIS PAPER. THANKS SO MUCH FOR YOUR HELP

Developed by Nancy Lange St. Clair. Reprinted with permission from Swap, S. (1987). *Enhancing parent involvement in schools.* New York: Teachers College Press, p. 56.

WILSON SCHOOL CLIMATE SURVEY: PARENTS

The purpose of this survey is to help the Wilson School to learn more about the attitudes of parents in order to improve the educational program. Your opinions and attitudes are very important. This is not a test; there are no right or wrong answers. We anticipate that it will take no more than ten minutes to complete this survey.

Before responding to the questions, please give us some information about yourself.

Number of children in the Boston Public Schools _____ Circle the Grades of children at Wilson   6   7   8

Circle the work that bestdescribes your race or ethnicity. Black, White, Asian/Pacific Islander, Hispanic, Native American

Zip Code _____

DIRECTIONS

The questions below describe a variety of conditions related to the Wilson School. We want to know to what extent you agree or disagree with each statement. Therefore, indicate your opinion by marking each statement as follows:
Circle the SA if you STRONGLY AGREE with the statement
     A if you AGREE but not strongly
     U if you are UNDECIDED
     D if you DISAGREE
     SD if you STRONGLY DISAGREE

EXAMPLE: The teachers at Wilson make me feel welcome when I visit the school.   SA   A   U   D   SD

••
••

1. I feel welcome whenever I visit the Wilson School.   SA   A   U   D   SD

2. The total educational program at Wilson is of high quality.   SA   A   U   D   SD

3. I make certain my child completes his/her homework.   SA   A   U   D   SD

4. I have visited the school more than 2 times this year.   SA   A   U   D   SD

5. The teachers at Wilson treat my child with respect.   SA   A   U   D   SD

6. The people in the principal's office care about my child.   SA   A   U   D   SD

7. I am proud of the Wilson School.   SA   A   U   D   SD

8. My child does not have enough homework.   SA   A   U   D   SD

9. The books my child uses in school are up to date.   SA   A   U   D   SD

10. The school provides enough activities so that everyone
    can find an activity to match his/her interest.   SA   A   U   D   SD

11. Discipline at the school is not consistent or fair.   SA   A   U   D   SD

12. I am aware of the responsibility of the School Parents Council.   SA   A   U   D   SD

13. The school has helped me and my child to set future educational
    goals.   SA   A   U   D   SD

14. The school meets the unique educational needs of my child.   SA   A   U   D   SD

15. The teachers encourage my child to do his/her best work.   SA   A   U   D   SD

Reprinted with permission from John Cawthorne, Department of Education, Boston College. For more information contact Roslyn Brown, Principal of the Wilson Middle School in Dorchester, MA.

Remember to circle the SA if you STRONGLY AGREE with the statement
A if you AGREE but not strongly
U if you are UNDECIDED
D if you DISAGREE
SD if you STRONGLY DISAGREE

16. I don't know anything about any parent groups at the school.   SA   A   U   D   SD

17. The school program is preparing students for the economic and
    social conditions of the 21st century.   SA   A   U   D   SD

18. Teachers call me about my child even when s/he is doing well.   SA   A   U   D   SD

19. I think my child was not very well prepared to enter middle school. SA   A   U   D   SD

20. I know how school-based management works at the Wilson School.   SA   A   U   D   SD

21. The teachers at Wilson don't really care about my child.   SA   A   U   D   SD

2. My child is not safe at the Wilson School.   SA   A   U   D   SD

23. If my child is having difficulty in school, I know who to call for
    him/her to get extra help.   SA   A   U   D   SD

24. The Wilson School is worse than most Boston Public Schools.   SA   A   U   D   SD

25. There is no drug or alcohol problem in the Wilson School.   SA   A   U   D   SD

END

****
****

For each of the three lists below, please put a "1" by the activity that you think is most important, a "2" by the second most important, a "3" by the third most important, and a "4" by the fourth most important.

LIST A	LIST B	LIST C
Parents volunteer in classrooms __	Parent workshops on dealing with teenagers ____	Parents should help with homework ____
Parents serve on school councils ____	Parent workshops on drug and alcohol abuse ____	Parents should only monitor homework ____
Parents attend parent-teacher conferences ____	Parent workshops on teen sexuality ____	Parents should "punish" children for not doing homework ____
Parents help design the curriculum __ _	Parent workshops on helping with children's homework ____	Parents should not interfere with homework ____

THANK YOU FOR YOU HELP. YOU WILL RECEIVE A COPY OF THE RESULTS WHEN THE FINAL REPORT IS COMPLETED.

APPENDIX D: SUGGESTED RESOURCES FOR REACHING OUT TO PARENTS WITH LIMITED ENGLISH PROFICIENCY

REACHING OUT TO IMMIGRANT FAMILIES

For immigrant families, especially when there are language barriers, drawing upon resources from the family's community may be helpful in establishing initial ties, providing information about organizations and agencies of importance in the community, or identifying individuals who could act as interpreters or speakers for parent meetings or staff training. Moreover, involving the cultural community sends a positive message about the school's interest in two-way communication with families. Expanding on a list developed by Siu,[1] some potential sources are

1. The sponsor of a refugee parent; a petitioner (relative) of a legal immigrant parent; refugee resettlement groups;
2. Other parents in the program who are from the same home country;
3. A preschool program in your area known for serving multicultural families;
4. The International Students office of your local college/university;
5. Foreign language department or social work/human service departments of your local college/university;
6. Ethnic places of worship or ethnic business establishments;
7. Language schools run by various ethnic groups;
8. National organizations advocating for refugees or immigrants;
9. Folk festivals or local ethnic museums.

Note. From Reaching out to culturally diverse families by S. Swap, In O. Moles (Ed.), *Schools helping urban parents strengthen home learning.* Washington, DC: Office of Educational Research and Improvement.

1. Siu, S. (1990). Where to start looking for resources in the community. (Unpublished handout available from the author, Wheelock College, 45 Pilgrim Road, Boston, MA 02215)

APPENDIX E: LISTENING IN A DIFFICULT SITUATION: A TRANSCRIPT

LISTENING RESPONSIVELY: ILLUSTRATIVE SCRIPT

A Parent–Teacher Dialogue Illustrating Effective Listening

Mrs. Green and Mrs. Davis are about to conclude their regularly scheduled conference about Bill. Bill is in the first grade and is making a good adjustment to this school. Although he has learning disorders, he is keeping up with the academic work and looks forward to school each day. Bill's mother has a concern related to the field trip and his food allergies that she feels she must mention before she leaves.

Mother: You know, Mrs. Davis, I still have some worries about the next field trip. I'm just not sure that everything is planned as well as it can be, and that it's going to be a good experience for Bill. I'm thinking that maybe I'll just keep him home. It would be easier for you, and then he'll be fine too.

Teacher: *Gee, I didn't realize. So you're worried about Bill's going on the field trip to the zoo with us.*

Mother: Well, there's so much that can happen. And I won't be there with him. How can you watch all those kids and then Bill with all those needs? What if, um, somebody has brought something on the bus that sets off an allergic reaction, for example, and he has trouble breathing? I think that really I better keep him home.

Teacher: *I see, so you're worried that something will happen to him.*

Mother: Oh, I'm terribly worried, but don't you think I have reason to be? I mean, he really has hardly gone anyplace without me, with a whole group. In his program last year, there were four teachers when he went anyplace, and they always carried medication. That way, if anything happened, he would be taken care of right away. This just seems so vague, in a big bus. I just don't think he's old enough to handle it.

Teacher: *What would make you feel comfortable, Mrs. Green?*

Mother: Well, I don't know. Maybe I should go. And then I could sit with him and be right on top of the situation. Um, but I don't think I could get the day off, and my mother could stay with him at home.

Teacher: *I see, so you feel that if somebody could be with him, watching him particularly, that would make you feel comfortable. Ideally, it would be you.*

Mother: Yeah, 'cause I know him so well: I know just how to take care of him. And I know how to read the signs. Before he starts to choke, he usually starts to breathe very fast, and I can tell when it's going to happen.

Note: From *Building Home-School Partnerships with America's Changing Families: An Instructional Kit* (pp. H17–H21) by L. Braun and S. Swap, 1987, Boston: Wheelock College. We are indebted to Phyllis Sonnenschein, Lexington, Massachusetts, for creating the role of the mother.

Teacher: So your main worry is that he's going to eat something he shouldn't eat. Is that what your main worry is?

Mother: Yeah, or there'll be some dust from the bus and he'll inhale it.

Teacher: So you have a lot of worries about this trip.

Mother: Oh, yeah, this trip is scary for me. He's just never been away with a group like this before.

Teacher: I see. But you would feel comfortable if you yourself were able to come and be with him and watch him.

Mother: Yeah. And I think he'd be happier too.

Teacher: I see.

Mother: It's not just that *I'm* worried. I think that he's probably . . . he hasn't said anything, but I think he's probably worried too, 'cause he hasn't really been without me that much. Here he is in a new school, um, and he's without me during the day, and the day's longer than it used to be. I think he would feel better if I were with him.

Teacher: So you think that going on the field trip would be scary for him.

Mother: Oh yes. I mean, has he said anything to you?

Teacher: No, he hasn't said anything to me at all about being scared about the field trip. As a matter of fact, when I showed the pictures of the animals, he pointed very excitedly and said, "Look at the elephants!"

Mother: (Smiling for the first time) Well, he loves animals. I would love him to go. But you know, maybe next year his class will go, and he'll be ready.

Teacher: Um hum. Well, let's think about it, and let's see if we can work out a way that you'll feel comfortable about it.

Mother: Well, do you see any solution? I mean is there any way to work it out if I can't come? Is there a person who could come and be with him, and I could explain all the things that I know, and sort of teach her what to do?

Teacher: Um, well, let's think about who might be available.

Mother: Well, I was really thinking of the nurse, because it's the medication and the breathing I worry about most.

Teacher: So obviously you think of the school nurse. Okay, so that's one possibility. Is there anybody else? What about your mother? You said your mother could babysit at home. Would she be available to come on the trip?

Mother: Yeah, right, maybe. She's kind of old to walk around all those animal paths. Maybe she could. I could ask her. I don't know. I didn't think of that.

Teacher: Well, would you like to ask her?

Mother: I'd kind of like him to go, 'cause, as you say, he did say something about all the animals he's going to see. And maybe he'd be able to feed some of them, and I'd like him to do it. And he feels so different anyhow, it would be a shame if he was the only one in the class. . . . What about some of the other kids who have trouble of one kind or another?

Teacher: Well, we're taking the whole group.

Mother: The whole class is going.

Teacher: And we are having two or three additional mothers who are coming. The school nurse is not coming. But if you would like to have your mother come, or possibly we could think of a teen-ager from the high school who would pay special attention to Bill. We could work that out.

Mother: Well, that would be good. Do you think this person could pay special attention and hold the medication, so that they could be ready to give it to him right away?

Teacher: I think we could take care of your concerns, yes.

Mother: Well, I'll think about it. When do I have to make up my mind?

Index

About the Author

Dr. Susan Swap received her B.A. from Radcliffe College and her Ph.D. in education and psychology from the University of Michigan in Ann Arbor. Currently she chairs the Department of Professional Studies and coordinates Professional Development School partnerships. She directs Wheelock's Center on Families, Communities, Schools, and Children's Learning, where a 5-year study is under way to explore how families of different ethnicities support their children's school achievement. Dr. Swap has been working with parents and educators for 20 years as a program developer, seminar leader, consultant, and researcher, and is active in her local community where her children are attending high school. Her other books include: *Enhancing Parent Involvement in School, Managing an Effective Inservice Program*, and with Linda Braun, *Building Home-School Partnerships with America's Changing Families: An Instructional Kit.*